THE MAGIC MAN IN THE SKY

EFFECTIVELY DEFENDING THE CHRISTIAN FAITH

CARL GALLUPS

 WND Books

DEDICATION

This book is dedicated to my precious wife, Pam. She is my childhood friend and sweetheart, my life-long companion, encourager, comforter, and the love of my heart. Her Christ-like living has been my inspiration for many years. Without her, the work of this book would have been utterly impossible.

CONTENTS

ACKNOWLEDGMENTS

I wish to extend my heartfelt gratitude to the following people who read, edited, and meticulously analyzed the initial manuscript. Their counsel, patience, and guidance have enabled me to bring this book to its final form. Their work was invaluable.

Dr. Fred Lackey, Assistant to the President
University of Mobile–Mobile, Alabama
Former President of the Alabama Southern Baptist State Convention
Senior Pastor, Westside Baptist Church, Jasper, Alabama
Author

Dr. William C. Gallups, Ph.D., Professor (retired)
Florida State University–Tallahassee, Florida
School of Business–Accounting/Auditing/Banking
Author

Dr. Dennis Brunet, Ph.D.
Senior Pastor, Midway Baptist Church–Midway, Florida
Adjunct Professor, New Orleans Baptist Theological Seminary

Dr. Joda Collins, Retired Pastor
   Evangelist, Author

Michael D. Shoesmith
   Author, researcher, journalist, Christian apologist, radio commentator, and entrepreneur–Ontario, Canada

SPECIAL WORDS OF THANKS

To you the reader, for reading my book and for reading this section even though you may not know these people. Without them, this book might not have been a reality.

A loving word of thanks is given to my mother, Holly, and my father, Bill, for always believing that I had something like this in me.

To the People of Hickory Hammock Baptist Church: they have patiently encouraged me, always believed in me, and ardently prayed for me. This book was written with their fervent love for the Word of God in mind.

Jerry McGlothlin, (President/CEO Specialguests.com) who stayed on me like a basketball coach, encouraging me on to "one more lap." He spoke up for this book and for me when others would not.

Ken Kaplan, (P.R. Specialist, video producer, entrepreneur, proud daddy of Angela Grace) who never stopped encouraging me, even in the toughest of times. Encouraging is his spiritual gift.

Dr. Grace Vuoto, (Executive Director, Edmund Burke Institute For American Renewal, Washington, D.C., media guest political commentator, and Editor of *Reflections* magazine) for graciously sharing her professional insight and suggestions. Her input was invaluable.

Jeff Kuhner, (Writer for the *Washington Times*, prominent radio talk show host, and media guest political commentator). He was an important source of inspiration and encouragement.

My Staff—Dr. Greg Robards, Rev. Jim Rinehart, Dr. Jack Goldfarb, Amie Morrell, Joanne Parker, Kimie Hamil, Jesse Stafford, and Ray Harper. Without them picking up a lot of slack, I would have never had the time to complete this work.

Parker Gallups, my grandson; his insatiable thirst to be proficient in the handling of God's Word and the ability to "always be ready to give an answer," was a deep inspiration for me to produce this work.

FOREWORD

Carl Gallups has created a work as unique as the man himself. The danger of studying biblical apologetics is that all too often it creates an environment as sterile and strange as a surgical room. Though vitally needed, these books tend to be complicated, rarely enjoyable, and more than a little intimidating. In *The Magic Man in the Sky*, Carl Gallups takes the reader into a real-world setting to which he can easily relate. The book flows, as does life, through the telling of a story.

The book will be a valuable asset to the reader because its tone and temper ring as true as the man himself. Carl Gallups is not some cloistered author who writes in the safe confines of his study. He is a strong defender of the faith, not only in the pulpit, but also in the public sector through radio, newspaper, and his website. Through the crucible of time and personal testing, the author has passionately embraced God's call to "...sanctify the Lord in your hearts: and be ready always to give an answer to every man that asketh you a reason of the hope that is in you with meekness and fear..." (1 Peter 3:15)

The Magic Man in the Sky is designed not for the professional scholar but for the salt-of-the-earth believer. The banner call is that every child of God can know the truth, and become strong and confident. Though deeply scriptural and splendidly sculptured along logic and science, the book is highly readable, and moves with grace while touching the heart. Without question, Carl has provided a valuable tool to inspire the people of God and to give hope to those lost in the confusion created by Satan and sin. I am honored to recommend this work.

May the Lord use it for His glory and the good of many.

—*Dr. Dennis J. Brunet*

I n *The Magic Man in the Sky* Carl Gallups has given us an exciting insight into the many unanswered questions of evolution theory and, based on biblical truths—both prophecies and promises, the possibilities of other worlds and realities denied by evolutionists. With his open and frank approach, supported by extensive research and information from learned professionals in their respective fields, Carl challenges believers and unbelievers to take a serious look at the subjects discussed in this book.

At the very heart and core of *The Magic Man in the Sky* is the challenge to approach each subject with an open mind, to be objective with each subject. Ultimately, Carl invites every reader to seriously consider the gravity and consequences of accepting or rejecting the truth presented.

In this hour of all-but-universal darkness, a bright ray of hope and confidence shines forth from the truths of this book. In a time when lives are marked by a growing hunger for spiritual realities, a hunger that cannot be satisfied with unanswered questions ignored and evaded by evolutionists, Carl Gallups, with remarkable ability and profound truths from Scripture, reveals the truth that real science and Holy Scripture are inseparably linked.

In this book, Carl verifies that behind all creation there is an Intelligent Designer who created all that exists. The Grand Designer controls it all and uses everything for His glory and the eternal good of all who acknowledge Him and serve Him through His Son Jesus Christ.

—*Dr. Fred Lackey*

VITAL QUESTIONS

- Can we prove the existence of God?

- Why are we here?

- Where are we going?

- What is the meaning of life?

- How is it possible that God exists—yet remains unseen?

- Does scientific evidence exist that supports the supernatural claims of the Bible?

- How can we be certain the Christian faith is the correct one?

- What about all the people who have never heard or will never hear the gospel?

- Why is our *worldview* so vital?

- Is evolution really a settled, scientific fact?

- What is the difference between an atheist and an agnostic?

- Can atheism be refuted with science and logic?

- Are we living in the *end times*?

- How does one refute a biblical antagonist?

- Can the Bible be trusted?

All of these questions, and many more, are soundly answered within the pages of this book. Enter and enjoy!

PROLOGUE

And be not conformed to this world: but be ye transformed by the renewing of your mind, that ye may prove what is that good, and acceptable, and perfect, will of God.
—Romans 12:2

RENEW YOUR MIND

Jesus Christ is Lord.

We proclaim these words and declare them as the core of our faith, but how do we defend this eternal truth in the face of today's thoroughly secular world?

Paramount to one's faith, Christians must know *what* they believe and *why* they believe it. Believers must be equipped and confident in defining the fundamental truths of our faith.

Two highly contradictory veins of thinking, *secularism* and *biblical truth*, characterize the times in which we live. Secularism sweeps into itself every philosophy that vainly stands up against the declarations of God's Word. By nature, secularism is atheistic to its very core. Quite naturally, these two worldviews are in a constant state of tension and antagonism. This tension is often expressed in the commonly used secularist idiom, "I would rather believe in settled scientific truth than to declare my belief in a mere *Magic Man in the sky*."

The foundational platform of the secularist's "settled scientific" worldview is that all living things began through an unpurposed evolutionary process without intelligent input. The premise of secularism is this: Since we live in an unplanned and randomly generated world, man is the ultimate *decider*, the ultimate authority. The secularist philosophy of life presents a world without God, without eternal meaning or direction, and, therefore, without eternal hope.

In this book, you will discover how to competently define and defend vital truths of science and Scripture. Perhaps then you will have augmented opportunities to lead an unbeliever to a saving faith in Jesus Christ. Few endeavors in life carry as much satisfaction.

Follow along, now, as we covertly drop in on a college campus. We will eavesdrop on two students, Christopher and Crowley, who are engaged in a conversation concerning their opposing worldviews.

Be prepared for your world to be jolted.

—*Carl Gallups*

· I ·

THE MAGIC MAN IN THE SKY

I don't believe in God for the same reasons that I don't believe in Mother Goose.
—Clarence Darrow, American Civil Liberties Union–Scopes trial lawyer, 1925

Christopher awoke early and set about preparing, in his usual manner, for another day at college. However, he was not equipped for the earth-shattering challenge he was about to encounter. Today would be a day of reckoning for Christopher's faith.

***

The midday sun injected its aureate beams of radiance across the commons of the small college campus. The two classmates walked side-by-side, having emerged from the student coffee shop only moments ago. The trees were just beginning to turn to their long-anticipated hues of October brilliance. The light breeze was cool and refreshing.

The two students sipped their steaming caffè latte. The day had a feel of heaven about it—in one manner of speaking, anyway.

As the current class period dismissed, the campus grounds swarmed with students. The young scholars moved from one academic appointment to another. A number of them were finished for the day but still milled around. An occasional screech of excitement and shout of recognition emanated from the continual flowing mass.

The two friends were each secretly anxious to reengage their conversation. Earlier, they had attempted to connect in a serious philosophical discussion. Their conversation had been interrupted, and they had postponed it for a more opportune time.

Christopher sincerely desired to lead his unbelieving classmate, Crowley, into a saving faith in Jesus Christ. He believed he might have made a little headway within his brief discussion. He had his classmate's attention and the possibility of further debate. The discussion had gone well, thus far.

Christopher thought that perhaps his friend, who pridefully claimed to be an atheist, was softening a bit. He prayed so. How wonderful if Christopher could report to his Christian friends the spiritual victory of leading an atheist to faith in the Lord. He felt a rush of excitement. He could not wait to begin the exchange.

However, Crowley was also eager to restart the dialogue. He believed he possessed the perfect answers for this naive advocate of the Christian Magic Man, as Crowley called Him. He readied himself to unleash his insight upon the seemingly gullible Christopher.

The two freshmen located a bench and sat together, sipping their coffee. They had a full twenty minutes left before their next class, so they engaged in a bit of small talk.

After a moment, Christopher took another swig from his steaming brew. As he swallowed it, he quickly collected his thoughts. He could not have known what hard-hitting arguments lay hidden within the mind of his atheist friend. The man of faith mustered up his nerve and plunged forward in conversation.

With guarded excitement, Christopher began, "I appreciate you speaking with me earlier today about my beliefs, Crowley. I hate that we were interrupted. I would really like to continue our conversation about the existence of God and His work of creation, if that's okay."

"Look, Christopher," said Crowley, with a sigh, "here is the crux of the whole matter for me. I, for one, would rather believe in the observable, proven, and settled scientific evidence concerning the origins and obvious evolution of life than in some magic man in the sky, as you Christians do. I don't believe in God for the same reasons that I don't believe in the tooth fairy," he shrugged.

"But wait a minute!" Christopher objected, "How can you accuse me of believing in a magic man in the sky? I haven't ever claimed such a thing. I think you're being unreasonable right from the beginning. You're suggesting that I believe in *magic*, and of all things—in a *fairy tale!*"

"But isn't that what you believe, when you get right down to it?" Crowley questioned. "You continually speak of the unseen and unobservable things that your God does. You talk about how He merely *speaks* things into existence. You talk about the mystical power of prayer and the magical, mystical Holy Spirit within you. You talk about Him living *up there*"—he tossed his head skyward—

"as if He were only a bigger and more powerful version of a man. In fact, you're often so vain as to refer to the human race as the crowning glory of His creation, as if humanity itself were the be-all and end-all of everything that exists. Millions of species of life exist, and yet you are so arrogant as to insist that humans are at the very top of this so-called *creation*. Isn't that true, Christopher?"

"Yes, well, but you don't . . . you don't understand. When I say those things, I . . . uh . . . that's not exactly what I mean—"

"And that's another thing," Crowley interrupted. "You *often* say things you don't mean. That's my point. Science declares only what it sees and what it has proven. It says what it means. Science deals only with the data that is before it. Scientific evidence has passed peer review and years of excruciating scrutiny. When a mistake is made, it is corrected. When new evidence is discovered, it is examined, tested, and published for all to reexamine. This is the true scientific process. And it makes much more rational and reasonable sense than your proclamations of *faith* in what your make-believe man in the sky has done."

"But you don't understand, Crowley," Christopher said, unnerved by the direction of this conversation. Time was bearing down on them. He rose, as did Crowley, and they started walking rapidly toward their next class. "You see, to believe in God," he began again, "*is* a matter of faith. You can't *prove* that He exists; you have to believe that He does. The Bible states this somewhere—the book of Hebrews, I believe. In order to please God, you must first believe He exists. I get my faith from the truth of the Bible as well as the wonders of creation. Therefore, my belief in God comes from my faith that He exists. It really is that simple."

"Yes, my friend. It is that *simple*," Crowley sighed, shaking his head in disbelief. "Don't you hear how foolish you sound? Listen to yourself! You are declaring that you are willing to believe in a God that you can't even see or prove. You can't see Him *do* anything. When He does do something, according to your definition of His activity, you declare it to be unexplainable and unobservable. You are ignoring the mountains of *observable* evidence and the work of brilliant scientists who agree on it. Are you willing to turn your back on the solid, logical data affirmed by the entire scientific community? You're willing to trade science and reason for faith in a magic man that you can't prove exists?

"Besides that, the Bible is just a book," he continued. "Simple and fallible men wrote it. Life, on the other hand, has now been proven scientifically to arise through the evolutionary process. The facts are in on these things, my friend. Evolution is settled science. How sad to hear you speak with such faulty logic and silliness."

"Well, yes . . . of course," Christopher stammered, "I suppose—when you put it like that . . . but . . ."

Sensing that Christopher was faltering, Crowley continued his assault. "How else *is* there to put it? Can you prove the existence of God? No, you can't. Can you verify that He created anything? No, you can't. Can you provide evidence that the scientific facts of today's understanding are incorrect and are somehow scientifically destroyed by the words in your *magic book* you call the Bible? Nope again. Besides, the presence of so much evil in the world is good enough proof for me that God does not exist. If an all-loving God did exist, evil would not.

"What about all the people in the world who have never heard the *magic message* from your *magic book*?" he went on. "Do you mean to tell me they are all going to hell? And what about all this stuff you're continually espousing about the *end of time* and the *last days*? Aren't you just trying to scare people into believing in your religion? How else *should* I put it?"

"Well, I know the Bible is the Word of God and that Jesus Christ is the Son of God and the Savior of humanity," Christo-

pher confidently responded. "I know we have a sin nature, and
we can't save ourselves. I know that—"

"*Listen* to yourself!" Crowley sputtered, interrupting again.
"You're merely reciting your religious doctrine to me. How do
you know any of that stuff is true? The only reason you believe it
is because you were raised that way. What if you were raised in a
different way or a far-away place of the world? What if you were
raised to believe in another religious system? I suppose you would
be as passionate about those beliefs as well. How can you say that
your religion is the only correct one? The world has hundreds of
religions. If you would just stop and listen to yourself every now
and then, you would be surprised how silly all that *Christian-ese*
sounds—truly unbelievable!"

"But . . . if you only knew what I know," Christopher pro-
tested. "If you could only see what I see, you wouldn't be so—"

"But I *don't* see what you see," Crowley cut in yet again. He
was good at that. "Here's the deal: my educated mind doesn't
work that way. When you can show me how real, observable,
and proven science supports your religion—I will listen. When
you can prove that your magic man in the sky really exists and
that your religion is the *right* one and the *only* one out of all the
others—then I will consider it. When you can explain to me how
all the scientists of the world can be so wrong and you and your
magic book can be so right, I might give it some thought. Until
then, we can be friends, but I don't want to discuss this absurd
matter any further."

Christopher shrugged his shoulders; exasperated, he turned
and walked away, his thoughts spiraling off into a murky mist.
Crowley manufactured a contented grin. He had another one
doubting his faith. He had accomplished his evangelistic work for
the day. While Christopher had left the verbal exchange confused
about his beliefs, Crowley left the conversation satiated.

DESPERATELY SEEKING ANSWERS

Two days later, determined to present Crowley's challenging questions to trusted leaders of his faith, he spoke with his pastor and his Sunday School teacher.

"Of *course* you can't *prove* the existence of God!" Pastor Jim explained. "You have to believe by faith. God has shown Himself to us. The Creation itself declares the existence of God. The Scripture is clear in this matter. Surely, you do not doubt your faith. You were raised better than that. I have known you since you were only a boy. You need to pray and read your Bible more. Engaging in conversations with hard-core atheists requires a lot of preparation. I told you that if you hung around those atheists long enough, especially that Crowley fellow, they would turn your brains to mush. Now you are starting to doubt your faith because of one muddled-up conversation with a confused pagan unbeliever. Here . . . let me pray for you."

With deep sincerity, the young man listened as his longtime and well-meaning pastor prayed for him, but his mind whirled with confusion. *"Perhaps my Sunday School teacher will have the answers,"* he thought.

***

"I'll tell you what you need," said Richard, a solid Christian and the teacher of Christopher's Sunday morning Bible class. "You need to set up a counseling appointment with Pastor Jim. And here . . . let me pray for you . . . "

As Christopher grasped his teacher's hand and listened to his prayer, his thoughts were distant and tangled.

I wonder . . . he thought. *Am I merely praying to a magic man in the sky?*

***

So, what do *you* think? Is Christopher's faith a futile one? Is his concept of God simply an imaginary *Magic Man in the sky?* Which student is correct in his understanding of life, science, and spiritual matters?

In the next chapter, you will discover the all-important difference that a person's worldview makes in how he approaches and understands the deep mysteries of life.

· 2 ·

THREE VIEWS OF LIFE

I am against religion because it teaches us to be satisfied with not understanding the world.
—Richard Dawkins, renowned atheist apologist and author

I hope life isn't a big joke, because I don't get it.
—Jack Handey, popular American humorist

Forgive, O Lord, my little jokes on Thee,
and I'll forgive Thy great big one on me.
—Robert Frost, "Cluster of Faith," 1962

In the final analysis, we find three major opposing worldviews. Everyone in the world, all seven billion of us, holds to one of these three worldviews in one way or another.

A *worldview* is a philosophy or a way of thinking about life. Our worldview affects everything we do—every judgment we make, every decision we make, every plan we implement, and every discussion in which we engage. It influences whom we marry, what we teach our children, how we do our jobs, and how we function as members of everyday society.

In light of these facts, it is vital to possess a thorough knowledge of the three dominating philosophies of life. They are the *secular worldview*, the *religious worldview*, and the *biblical worldview*.

The *secular worldview* is a philosophy of life that altogether denies the existence or the necessity of God. This view is a thoroughly materialistic understanding of life. The secularist holds hard to the proposition that evolutionary theory is the singular explanation for the existence of life.

This philosophy declares that humankind is the highest determiner of all that is true and right. The *individual* is deemed the sole authority that determines good and evil, right and wrong, legal and illegal, for him or her self. The philosophy denies, ignores, or dismisses the reality of the spiritual realm or the moral absolutes of God's Word.

Within this paradigm of secular thought, most attempts to discuss the spiritual possibilities of life are frequently replaced with the latest discoveries of science. These discoveries are then presented as the ultimate realities and truths. This was the view of the atheist, Crowley, in chapter 1. For him, to believe in anything spiritual is like believing in a *Magic Man in the sky* or the tooth fairy.

Secularism is the worldview of the atheist, the evolutionist, and the majority of agnostics. I will speak much more about these groups of people in subsequent chapters.

The *religious worldview* is not much better than the secular, except that it at least acknowledges the reality of the spiritual or supernatural aspects of life. Several billion people live according to this particular worldview. This philosophy of living encompasses all manner of *religiosity*, everything from Wicca and Satanic occultism to the more than 250 religious systems and subsystems of the world. This particular paradigm of belief also encompasses the New Age movement with its several tentacles, including the UFO craze. In short, the religious worldview gladly accepts the reality of the spiritual or supernatural elements of life, but with one fatal flaw: it categorically denies that Jesus Christ is Lord and the *exclusive way* to salvation.

The *biblical worldview* measures life primarily through the revealed truth of the Word of God—the Bible. Contrary to the belief of some, this view of life is not afraid of science, especially science that is verified through the rigorous application of applied scientific method. In fact, this worldview actively seeks such scientific understanding of life.

While various methods of interpreting certain controversial passages within the Bible abound, the fact remains that the biblical understanding of life stands uniquely apart from the other two views. The biblical worldview can be summarized as follows:

1. The God of the Bible is the sovereign Creator of the universe. Without the existence of God, we have no life—anywhere. The various original life forms, or as the Bible calls them, *kinds*, including humankind, were made by the direct creative acts of God. The living descendants of any of the original *kinds* may be represented in various species of today's world. This fact reflects the inherent genetic potential within the original kinds. Only limited biological changes have naturally occurred within each type of living thing since the original Creation.

2. All of creation is in a fallen state of sin and depravity. It is this fallen state that accounts for the evil and ills that abound in our world. We call this understanding the doctrine of *original sin*. Man can do nothing to save himself from his lost and depraved condition. Because of our sin nature, we are out of perfect fellowship with our Creator. Man is intrinsically selfish, with only the occasional capacity to practice true and selfless morality.

3. God has provided man's salvation through the atoning work of Jesus Christ on Calvary's cross. Jesus' resurrection from the dead is proof that His work is real and that His work is now complete. Our greatest need is salvation from our sin nature and restoration to a right relationship with our Creator. That salvation is solely dependent upon what we do with Jesus' exclusive claim upon our life.

4. Through His Word, God reveals to us His holy nature and character. Through this revelation of God's holy character, we derive our understanding of true morality, including *absolute* morality. *Absolute morality* is defined as: those moral virtues that are *always* true regardless of the times or cultures in which we live. Absolute morality transcends man's whimsical and changing ideas of what is right and what is wrong.

5. Through the preceding four foundational understandings, we formulate our views of life and morality. From them, we also determine our understanding of how a home, marriage, church, nation, and society ought to function.

From these revealed truths, we understand that the evolutionary proposition of the *origin of life* is antithetical to God's truth. Through the biblical worldview, we further understand that activities and philosophies such as homosexuality, fornication, abortion, and moral relativism, for example, are wrong—God calls them *sin*.

The biblical worldview causes us to recognize that there *are* moral imperatives. There *are* moral absolutes, and we are accountable to God for our moral actions. From our understanding of these truths, and other truths like them, we formulate our pattern for life and the decisions we make regarding life's direction.

A QUICK REVIEW

The secular worldview is a view without an eternal and accountable moral compass. It proclaims that the human race alone is the ultimate determiner of right and wrong. The secularist sees no need for God. *We* are the center of the universe. We are here because of the mere happenstance of randomness. Evolution is the vehicle by which life arrived upon our planet.

In the religious worldview, spirituality is at least recognized, and manufactured religions are designed to deal with the myriad of religious and spiritual appetites that humanity possesses. Like the secular worldview, this conception of the world is also human-centered. It merely elevates man's sinful nature to a more religious plane of discussion while avoiding a personal accounting to a sovereign Creator. Moreover, it denies that Jesus is the *exclusive way* of salvation and restoration to God. Satan is the ultimate constructive force behind the religious worldview.

The biblical worldview centers upon the existence of the Creator God and our accountability to Him. God is the highest of all deciders and the giver of life. Out of the nature of God's character flows all knowledge of what is ultimately right and wrong. Life is sacred; life is cherished, but God is the ultimate reality. He alone is the center of all that is truth.

Within one of these three worldviews—secular, religious, or biblical—lies the philosophical foundation of every human being who is capable of thought and function.

Every person and every society will decide upon a worldview or philosophical paradigm in which to operate. On occasion, people and/or societies will move through paradigm shifts or philosophical changes regarding the path of life they choose. The shift, however, will always adjust between one of these three: the secular, the religious, or the biblical worldview.

The greatest divisiveness reveals itself between two of these three worldviews. I call this division the *great divide*. In the next chapter, we will take the plunge into that cavernous partition.

· 3 ·

THE GREAT DIVIDE

One might ask, "Since the biblical worldview *is* a religious worldview, why is it not merely included in the category of 'religious'? Why is it separate? Is its exclusion not just an overt prejudice on the part of the author?" These are fair questions. They are also questions of eternal significance. Moreover, their *answers* are of eternal significance.

Biblical Christianity is not a mere religion. *Religion* can be defined as humanity's imaginative attempt to make spiritual sense of the world around them. Therefore, religion involves our own self-centered endeavors to work out our eternal nature and our eternal destiny. Thus, the world is bursting with religions because society is full of ideas on how our destiny should be accomplished. Satan is more than eager to assist the human's quest for a merely religious endeavor.

Consequently, one religious devotee dances around a fire and beats tom-toms; another hugs a tree and sings to it; while yet another rubs the belly of a fat man molded into a golden statue. Some kneel on a prayer rug several times a day, facing Mecca, and adhere to strict rules and laws. Others search out an esoteric plane of spiritual existence by getting in touch with their inner *spirit-man* through a series of spiritual and mental gyrations. In each of these examples, the individual attempts to connect with his or her spiritual nature through a means that is *personally* contrived.

On the other hand, biblical Christianity is a universe apart from 250-plus religious systems that various civilizations have devised. Christianity is not defined as an *individual reaching up to* God in an effort to connect with his or her spiritual nature. Rather, it defines itself as *God reaching down to humankind,* taking it upon Himself to save us from our fallen spiritual condition. God reached down to us at enormous expense to Himself. The motivation for God's action is His love for us. There is no real comparison between Christianity and the systems of a merely religious nature.

"But," one might ask, "how do we know that Christianity is the only correct way for man to truly connect with his Creator?" This is another fair question.

The central message of Christianity is that the Creator of the universe is actively working to redeem fallen humanity back to Himself. What separates Christianity a universe apart from all other faith expressions is that, in order to accomplish the task, God Himself became a man, in the person of Jesus Christ, and through Jesus provided the sacrifice for our sin nature. After doing this, Jesus rose from the grave, alive, to prove that He alone is the Lord of life, the Author of life, and the Giver of eternal life.

The biblical message also declares that man is accountable to God, who provides us the means for our eternal salvation. We have the choice of believing Him and loving Him, or rejecting Him. He will not force Himself upon us. The decision is ours. Nothing else in *all* the world or all of history comes close to this astounding reality. The biblical message stands in a category unto itself.

However, the fact that Christianity stands exclusively apart from all of the merely fabricated religions does not necessarily make it the only correct belief system, though it does demand that Christianity be examined for its obvious uniqueness. Once Christianity is divided out from every other faith statement, it becomes the particular dividing point of worldviews. The unique message of the biblical faith is what singularly causes the *great divide*.

Understanding this great divide, then, assists us in the continuation of our discussion. For the two worldviews that, without a doubt, must collide with the mightiest clash are the worldviews of secularism and biblical Christianity. These two value systems are polar opposites in the classrooms, government halls, scientific laboratories, religious institutions, and the societal discussions of today's world.

When these philosophies collide, we can expect an explosion. Someone's paradigm of life teeters when the dust settles. We observed these two views colliding in chapter 1. Our atheist antagonist comes from the secular worldview. Crowley's *god* is science. His *bible* is whatever declaration of life the prevailing science decides. Down through the ages, the secular worldview has adjusted its truth numerous times. It does this because it sits upon shifting sand.

The ultimate nemesis to the secularist's god is the God of the Bible, because He claims sovereignty over the god of secular science—and any other *god*. The God of the Bible claims that He is the Author of all that is true, and that without Him, life cannot exist.

The god of the secular atheist (evolution postulation) insists that we have no need for the God of the Bible. Science, the atheist declares, has life all figured out. The secularist claims that his faith can be placed in the latest teachings of modern science. All the while, he seemingly forgets that science, over the centuries, has failed us and embarrassed us countless times. Its truths have been tweaked, adjusted by deceit, and *scrapped* on numerous occasions during our historical journey.

In spite of these dubious facts of science and history, the secularist declares with great confidence that life is possible without the need for the Intelligent Designer who has presented Himself within the pages of the Bible. To the secularist, the Bible is merely a book of ancient fairytales.

These are the two worlds that collide with the loudest debate. Our journey continues as we scrutinize them through the lens of true scientific evidence and the truth of the Word of God.

· 4 ·

THE NON-ANSWER

"True truth is always the truth—no matter how it is determined."

The story is told of a helicopter pilot who was flying the skies above a major metropolitan center. During his flight, an electrical malfunction disabled all of the aircraft's navigation and communication equipment. In addition, the sky was growing dark, and the fog was beginning to thicken. Navigation was quickly becoming impossible. Within minutes, the pilot had no idea where he was in relation to the airport.

Just in time, he noticed a tall building with several bright lights shining from within. He flew through the dense fog toward the well-lit building, the chopper blades frantically grabbing the air and punctuating it with their rhythmic beating.

The pilot suddenly had a clever idea. He instructed the single passenger to draw a handwritten sign. The passenger eagerly complied.

The sign read *WHERE AM I?*, and the passenger was directed to wave the sign in the helicopter's window so the building's occupants would clearly see it. The pilot inched the chopper as close to the building as he could safely get.

As fortune would have it, several people inside the building began peering through the windows of the skyscraper. They were captivated by the obviously disoriented helicopter, but alarmed by the chopper's close proximity to their building.

One man grabbed binoculars from his desk and quickly surveyed the situation outside. Seeing the scrawled, makeshift sign that was being held up by the aircraft's passenger, he instructed the others who were with him to gather the necessary items with which to respond.

One person was also charged with the responsibility of signaling with her hands and performing her best act of charades to assure those in the helicopter that an answer to their question would soon be on its way.

The pilot was tremendously relieved, believing that if he just knew the location of *this* specific building, he could perhaps obtain his bearings and chart a course to the airport. He anxiously waited as the fog grew thicker, and the night grew darker. His passenger grew more nervous as the moments passed.

At last, the folks in their high-rise offices were back with their poster and their answer. Hopefully, it would provide the clue to the pilot's safe course to the airport.

The building's occupants held up a large sign, well displayed in a brightly lit window. Their answer to the question *WHERE AM I?* hand-printed in large red letters read, "YOU ARE IN A HELICOPTER!"

The pilot smiled, waved, looked at his map, determined the course to steer to the airport, and went to it—straightaway. He then landed the helicopter safely, to the immense satisfaction of his scarcely breathing passenger.

After they were on the ground, the breathless passenger asked the pilot how the YOU ARE IN A HELICOPTER sign had helped determine their position. The pilot responded, "Well, from their answer I knew they had to be in the Acme Telecommunications Customer Support building. I knew this because they gave me a technically correct but entirely useless answer. Using that building as a reference point, I then flew straight to the airport."

The secular worldview often provides the same type of instructions to a world of people wandering in the fog of life.

The worldview that leaves God out of the picture, on occasion, can come up with technically correct observations. *True truth* is always truth—no matter how it is determined. However, while ignoring the Word of the *Creator* of all true truth, even technically correct information can render a useless answer. This is particularly critical when the information and answer are necessary for determining eternal consequences.

A simple example of this dichotomy would be the basic declaration of evolutionary theory. Evolution states that *specia tion* (the process by which individual species undergo certain identifiable physical changes over time) is an observable, scientific phenomenon, and that speciation occurs through the process of *natural selection*. Natural selection is the process by which living organisms *naturally* change over time as certain physical traits are *selected* over other physical traits due to environmental factors or genetic transferences.

By observing speciation, the evolutionist surmises that evolution involving one species eventually becoming another species accounts for the *total variation* of life that we now observe. Therefore, the evolutionist would argue: we have no need for God or an Intelligent Designer now that we have proven the fact of speciation.

Limited speciation is a technical truth and a scientifically proven fact. Man has observed certain changes, over time, within various species of living things. A number of these changes occur through breeding and genetic transference. Still other changes, on occasion, come because of environmental factors. The enlightened Christian would not deny these proven and observable facts.

However, this piece of accurate information does not even come close to proving that we have no need of an Intelligent Designer. In fact, the creation scientist would argue the opposite. Because when a small change takes place *within* a species—the species always remains a certain *kind*. This truth may more accurately reveal an embedded, intelligent coding system within that *particular* living thing's genetic makeup.

In other words, dogs are always dogs, regardless of how many various species of the dog exist. Dogs never become another *kind* of living thing. There are several variations of horses and cats, as well. Yet, horses and cats are always horses and cats. In addition, the latest DNA evidence powerfully suggests that humans have always been humans, and chimps have always been chimps—in spite of evolution's insistence that the two somehow relate through a *common ancestor*. Unfortunately for the evolutionist, that elusive common ancestor has never been confirmed or discovered, although this does not stop the insistence that one exists—somewhere. So, rather than proving that an Intelligent Designer does not exist, the scientific fact of speciation serves as strong evidence of an intricate and intelligent coding process—*predetermined* by an Intelligent Designer.

The creationist would also argue that speciation is a process that apparently *knows* how to bring about certain changes within a species while at the same time preserving genetic *locks*, ensuring that one *kind* of life cannot become another kind of life. Evolution's *origins theory* declares as fact that one kind of life actually becomes another kind of life through speciation, over millions of years. Nevertheless, *origins theory* has yet to scientifically demonstrate that this process has actually occurred.

Limited and occasional speciation is a scientific fact. However, this fact alone does not address the question of the existence of God and how His existence affects our lives and eternal future.

The secular worldview often holds up a hastily produced placard in the window of life. The poster sometimes possesses a technically correct answer to several essential questions—yet the answer, in reality, is useless in determining the ultimate direction or meaning of life.

Luckily, the helicopter pilot was smart enough to find his direction from the answer he had been given. He merely recognized the absurdity of the *self-impressed* source from whence it came and took the tidbit of truth the source did provide to formulate his life-saving plan. Frequently, the Christian finds himself in a similar position as he moves through this secular and often befuddled world.

The conflict between these two worldviews, the secular and the Christian, regularly results in the biggest of explosions. Now let us examine what happens when these two worlds collide.

· 5 ·

WHEN TWO WORLDS COLLIDE

"[Evolution] has resulted in traits such as group selfishness being coded in our genes."
—Dr. Christian de Duve, biochemist and 1974 winner of the Nobel Prize for Physiology or Medicine

A few pages back, I mentioned the concept of *true truth*. This is a vital notion. We have *truth,* which modern science often declares with confidence. Much of the time, the declaration of that *truth* turns out to be *true truth,* but at times, it does not. Every now and then, a declaration of *truth* turns out to be *momentary* truth. Between *true truth* and *momentary truth is a world of difference!*

Examples: At one point in history, the brilliant minds of the world declared that the earth was flat. A number of great minds proclaimed that the world was held up at the four corners by giant elephants. This was declared as truth. Others thought the sun revolved around the earth. To believe anything different was considered unscientific, to the point of absurdity.

For eons, men believed that if one sailed upon the seas long enough, one would reach the end of the world and then tumble over the edge. At one time, all of these concepts were declared as *truth*, and they were thought to be truth because the enlightened minds and the scientists of their time *said so*. As we now know, they were not true. In fact, they were not even close to the truth.

Nevertheless, *true truth* is always the truth.

Learned men declared for the longest time that *spontaneous generation* (living matter spontaneously arising out of nonliving matter) was fact. They proclaimed this theory as truth since they had observed the emergence of living organisms (maggots, for example) seemingly out of nowhere from nonliving material. Spontaneous generation was declared as one of the scientific answers concerning the origins of life. This position was solidified by Aristotle and held grip on the scientific world for almost two thousand years. Observe Aristotle's own words on this matter:

> "So with animals, some spring from parent animals according to their kind, whilst others grow spontaneously and not from kindred stock; and of these instances of spontaneous generation some come from putrefying earth or vegetable matter, as is the case with a number of insects, while others are spontaneously generated in the inside of animals out of the secretions of their several organs."[1]

"Animals and plants come into being in earth and in liquid because there is water in earth, and air in water, and in all air is vital heat so that in a sense all things are full of soul. Therefore living things form quickly whenever this air and vital heat are enclosed in anything. When they are so enclosed, the corporeal liquids being heated, there arises as it were a frothy bubble."[2]

Aristotle (384–322 BC) was a Greek philosopher, a student of Plato, and the teacher of Alexander the Great. How remarkable that Aristotle is still considered one of the most significant founding figures in Western philosophy and science. Yet, this astounding thinker and scientist was wrong on the matter of spontaneous generation—he *was* wrong concerning the fundamental question of life.

This is no small error. His massive miscalculation went to the foundation of life itself. Yet, anyone who wished to argue for the spontaneous generation of life, and the absence of a need for God, could have appealed to the *truth* of Aristotle. After all, he possessed a scientific mind of astounding proportions, and his postulate was taken for granted to be truth. Nevertheless, Aristotle was wrong.

Not until the nineteenth century, when Louis Pasteur expanded upon the earlier works of others who had begun research into the matter, did we discover and prove that spontaneous generation was a scientific impossibility. Aristotle's theory turned out to be little more than sheer superstition. *Germ theory* and *cell theory* replaced the disproved spontaneous generation. Now, one would be considered superstitious and/or ignorant if he believed that something living could appear by *magic* from something that, up until that time, was nonliving. On the other hand, would he really be considered ignorant—today? With no apparent shame, modern-day scientists have dusted off the understanding of *spontaneous generation*. In the late 1800s, a new, shined-up, spiffed-up, spun-about name was given to the term. The revised expression was—abiogenesis. Evolutionists could start over, without the negative press earned by the term's predecessor. I will discuss this in much further detail in subsequent chapters. For the sake of our understanding of *true truth*, however, let me deal with it here in a light way.

Today, abiogenesis is the foundational cornerstone of *origins theory*. In denial of the need for an intelligent designer, abiogenesis, even after nearly 150 years, is the best that modern science has to offer in the way of explaining the origins and supposed evolution of millions of species of life. Abiogenesis, unbelievably, is still the modern scientific explanation of how life arose from previously nonliving matter. In reality, it is merely the unscientific, ancient, and superstitious idea of spontaneous generation. Even so, evolutionists and atheists, with immense pride, declare it to be—modern *truth*.

Today's explanation of abiogenesis attempts to clean up the untidy little fact of its unempirical nature. Evolution scientists do this by declaring that spontaneous generation of life from nonlife occurred only *once,* and in only one organism, but eventually *diversified* (through evolution) from that one organism. In other words, the evolutionist insists that it is a settled *truth* that all of life, as we now comprehend it, all several million forms, arose from a singular *common ancestor.* They say this common ancestor arose *spontaneously* (a proven scientific impossibility) from nonliving matter. This is today's truth. Something tells me this is not *true truth*. What say you? Now you understand how worldviews collide. The collision revolves around truth. The question is this: are we speaking of *momentary* truth—or *true truth*? This is a consideration of eternal significance.

THE COLLISION

A collision of worldviews is not a new phenomenon. From the beginning of time, the biblical worldview and secularism have had contradictions.

God created Adam and Eve with the innate ability to understand His truth. Their view of the world and life was God-centered. In their original form, they walked and communicated with God, in person.

The Bible reveals that Satan, the adversary, deceitfully removed the clarity that God gave them and convinced Eve to see things through a window of self-centeredness. The very words of God were called into question: *"Did God really say . . . ?"*

God was reduced, in Satan's argument, to a selfish Magic Man in the sky who did not want Eve to become like Him—once she knew *good and evil.*

The introduction of that worldview, in the end, led to destruction. From Eve's self-destruction, the deception of the secular worldview has been forever passed down to humankind through the ages. Of course, this is ancient news.

A biblical worldview, on the other hand, begins with Creation as it is revealed in the first two chapters of Genesis. It continues with the understanding that the principles and precepts of the first eleven chapters of Genesis are given to us to be interpreted in a literal sense.

These first eleven chapters form the foundation of the whole of the Christian faith. Satan knows this. I believe this is the precise reason the biblical presentation of life in these chapters, from the Creation to the Flood, is vehemently disputed by the secular teachings of evolution and the atheistic worldview.

The secular paradigm of life presses hard against the biblical model of life. We should not be surprised, then, to discover that a number of people who claim to be of the Christian faith are now questioning the literal nature of the Creation events revealed in the Bible. Some have even embraced a form of evolution understanding within their worldview.

After the Creation account, the next foundation of the biblical worldview is an understanding of the fall of man and his subsequent need for redemption. We call this fallen condition *depravity*. Humankind is lost, without hope, in its sin.

The secular worldview proclaims that each of us is a moral being from within our very makeup. It declares that humanity is basically *good*. We commit evil deeds *only* because we do not have adequate education, or enough money, or because someone else has harmed us or influenced us in a negative manner.

In contrast, the biblical worldview declares the observed *true truth*—we are sinners from birth. If you have ever been around a small child, you understand this to be a fact. An infant soon learns that if it persistently cries, at just the right volume, it will become the center of attention. It believes its immediate needs should be the focus of the entire universe. Some, in humor, (but declaring a clear observation of truth) call this self-centered condition of the human infant a *viper in a diaper.*

As the child becomes a toddler, we soon discover that we do not have to teach him to be dishonest or selfish. He was born that way. We must then spend several years of our child's life fervently attempting to teach him to be honest, truthful, self-sacrificing, and focused on the bigger picture of life. I have yet to be acquainted with a toddler that is honest to the core, selfless, and nondemanding. That tot does not exist. Why is this? Because the total condition of the human being is fallen. It is self-seeking—in whole. The human family possesses a collective sin nature. The Bible declares this truth in clear fashion. The secular worldview often illogically denies this plain truth as though it does not exist.

The one who holds to *scriptural truth* as his worldview recognizes that we live in a fallen world. We live in a stunningly beautiful creation that nonetheless bears the unmistakable marks of the curse of sin and the rejection of God's truth. Scripture teaches that all are sinful (Romans 3:23). We will do evil things unless we are restrained by law and ultimately redeemed by God's salvation offered through Jesus Christ.

The Word of God reveals that the most desperate need of the human race is not a better environment, a little bit of encouragement, more money, a higher education, or a new and shiny government program. The biblical worldview proclaims that sin (the rejection of God's way, Word, and will) is the source of all of our problems, and the only true answer is a spiritual regeneration of life through Christ.

Ironically, the secularist's worldview sees a dire necessity to save the planet's ecology but ignores the salvation of the souls and lives of the lost *people* who live on that planet. In secularism, a person is declared a hero if she participates in saving dolphins, or trees, or manatees, but is declared a villain and an outlaw if she commits her life to saving babies from bloody and violent abortions. Similarly, a person can be imprisoned for molesting eggs in the nest of an eagle or a turtle, but will receive federal assistance and police protection while mutilating a human child within the womb.

The secular worldview declares that homosexuality, fornication, and adultery are *natural* and, therefore, acceptable parts of the human experience. It goes as far as to declare that society's laws must protect these activities. All the while, the devastating effects of each of these perverse activities have been observed and cataloged since time immemorial.

In the final analysis, then, in the secular worldview, the creation is worshipped more than the Creator. This truth was declared over two thousand years ago in Paul's treatise to the Romans:

Professing themselves to be wise, they became fools, and changed the glory of the uncorruptible God into an image made like to corruptible man, and to birds, and fourfooted beasts, and creeping things. Wherefore God also gave them up to uncleanness through the lusts of their own hearts, to dishonour their own bodies between themselves: who changed the truth of God into a lie, and worshipped and served the creature more than the Creator, who is blessed for ever. Amen. (Romans 1:22–25)

When a culture is saturated with and immersed in a secular worldview, *social justice* becomes the magical answer to all of man's tribulations. Political activity and government programs take the place of spiritual transformation and regeneration. A feel-good, self-help, self-esteem-worshipping philosophy springs up around this view and makes its way into the culture and, over time, into the preaching from some pulpits.

A *more positive gospel* that denies the revulsion of sin and humanity's desperate need for redemption begins to tickle the ears of a deluded citizenry. Sin is no longer declared the ultimate problem. The human dilemma is relegated to the mere *lack of opportunity*.

As you can now see, the worldview you choose and the lens through which you look will determine how you perceive all of life. If the prescription of your lens is not correct, nothing will be in focus. Who knows? Looking through this distorted lens, one might believe that we are merely an unplanned cosmic accident, the result of random happenings, with no rhyme or reason and no purpose or plan. We may even believe there is no eternity and no accountability for our actions in this life. If we choose to believe these things, then we are subscribing to the secular worldview. If you subscribe to the secular worldview, your life will be lived with its exclusive purpose being to *survive*.

However, if your worldview is based on the Word of God, then you will understand that you are not a mere accident. You will be assured that your life has purpose, dignity, and value—eternal value. You will also understand that you are accountable for your actions and that the living of your life, here and now, reflects upon your eternity. Additionally, you will humbly understand that you are utterly depraved and without hope other than through the redeeming grace of God offered through Jesus Christ.

At the beginning of chapter 2, I included a quote by Dr. Richard Dawkins, a renowned evolutionist and atheist apologist. He stated, "I am against religion because it teaches us to be satisfied with not understanding the world."

Now that you have looked through the lens of the biblical worldview, you can discern that nothing could be farther from the truth. In fact, it is the *secular* worldview that teaches us to not be satisfied with understanding the world and the *true truth* that governs it. We are not to even consider our eternal nature or the God who created us. Instead, the secularist proclaims, we are to ignore God and live exclusively by the rules of secular humanism. Sad to say, many choose this route and lose themselves in darkness and fog. Many times they can catch a glimpse of truth, but eternal and *true truth* often eludes them. Another irony of the secular worldview is worth noting. Secular humanists are forced to borrow from a *biblical worldview* to explain what can be plainly observed about the human condition and its obvious innate nature of total selfishness (sin). Consider the theory given by Dr. Christian de Duve, a biochemist of international acclaim and professor emeritus at New York City's Rockefeller University. He is also the 1974 winner of the Nobel Prize for Physiology or Medicine. His observations are duplicated here from a portion of an interview in *New Scientist* magazine concerning the *problem of humanity*.[3]

Remember that Dr. de Duve is a decided advocate of evolution and the secular worldview. Following is one way the secularists attempt to grapple with the observable problem of "sin." The title of the article is: "Natural Selection Will Destroy Us." (Keep in mind that "natural selection" means *evolution*.)

New Scientist: You think that natural selection has worked against us. How?

Dr. de Duve: Because it has no foresight. Natural selection has resulted in traits such as group selfishness being coded in our genes. These were useful to our ancestors under the conditions in which they lived, but have become noxious to us today. What would help us preserve our natural resources are genetic traits that let us sacrifice the present for the sake of the future. You need wisdom to sacrifice something that is immediately useful or advantageous for the sake of something that will be important in the future. Natural selection doesn't do that; it looks only at what is happening today. It doesn't care about your grandchildren or grandchildren's grandchildren.

New Scientist: You call this shortsightedness "original sin," Why did you pick this terminology?

Dr. de Duve: I believe that the writers of Genesis had detected the inherent selfishness in human nature that I propose is in our genes, and invented the myth of original sin to account for it. It's an image. I am not acting as an exegete—I don't interpret scripture.

New Scientist: How can humanity overcome this "original sin"?

Dr. de Duve: We must act against natural selection and actively oppose some of our key genetic traits.

New Scientist: One solution you propose is population control, but isn't this ethically dubious?

Dr. de Duve: It is a simple matter of figures. If you want this planet to continue being habitable for everyone that lives here, you have to limit the number of inhabitants. Hunters do it by killing off the old or sick animals in a herd, but I don't think that's a very ethical way of limiting the population. So what remains? Birth control. We have access to practical, ethical and scientifically established methods of birth control. So I think that is the most ethical way to reduce our population.

Did you get that? According to de Duve, the human race possesses many *noxious* (deadly) traits, like *group selfishness* (sin). He says these traits are coded in our DNA. He further insists that they will be our undoing unless *we* can fix them. Natural selection (evolution) is *shortsighted* (it has missed the mark) in *allowing* for this *original sin.* Therefore, man must come up with his own solution to his original sin. And that solution, concludes de Duve, is *population control.* Here is the real problem: the world is in a fog, flying in a helicopter on a dark and stormy night. The secular worldview has just held up the placard in the window of their ivory tower, proclaiming the answer for life. They have parts of the answer technically correct. However, their overall directions are useless for eternity's sake, for humankind *is* depraved beyond hope. We *do* have a coded sin nature within us. We are incapable of and helpless in correcting the problem ourselves. Ten thousand years of human history have borne out this fact. The solution is not population control, but rather, a healing of the heart and mind.

This *soul healing* is accomplished only when a person is born again by the Holy Spirit of God through a personal relationship with Jesus Christ. Only our Creator can accomplish the internal task of covering our sin nature. And He has done so, through

His Son. The Word of God declares that our sin problem was atoned for (covered) on Calvary's cross:

> For God sent not his Son into the world to condemn the world; but that the world through him might be saved. He that believeth on him is not condemned: but he that believeth not is condemned already, because he hath not believed in the name of the only begotten Son of God. And this is the condemnation, that light is come into the world, and men loved darkness rather than light, because their deeds were evil. (John 3:17–19)

The secular worldview does not have realistic and cohesive positions on the deepest questions of life. Neither does it provide sufficient answers for the existence of knowledge, logic, or ethics. If we are merely a ball of chemicals and electrical impulses, collected at random and spontaneously generated, then how do we satisfactorily answer these questions: *Who am I? Why am I here? How am I supposed to live, and who decides that for me?* The worldly answer is, "You are an accidental generation of chemicals with no eternal purpose. Live as it pleases you—the best you can. This life is all there is. Just do your best to survive."

Furthermore, the secular worldview cannot, with any degree of reason, answer, *"Why do I have the ability to think, create, design, feel, and disseminate information to the rest of the world around me? If I am an accidental, random hodgepodge of chemical conjoining, why do I* want *to ponder and invent and communicate—and why am I the only species who does these things intentionally, and not just instinctively?"*

And the secularist responds, *"You are flying in a fog in a helicopter."* Gee. Thanks.

Nevertheless, rest assured, the biblical worldview has logical, reasonable, and scientifically verified answers to all of these questions.

***

The story is related of a pompous college freshman who was attending a raucous football game. Seated beside him was a senior citizen, and the two began conversing. As they talked, the pretentious youth began to explain to his elder why it was impossible for the older generation to understand his younger and more enlightened generation.

"You grew up in such a different world. Actually, your world was almost a primitive one," the student declared, loud enough for many of those nearby to hear. "The young people of today grew up with satellite TV, jets, space travel, and man walking on the moon. Our space probes have visited Mars. We have nuclear energy, electric and hydrogen cars, computers with light-speed processing, cell phones, and all manner of electronic convenience and communication modes, and . . ." The long-winded young man paused to take a huge gulp of his soft drink.

Taking advantage of this break in the student's wordy litany, the elderly gentleman proclaimed, "You know what? You are right, son. We did not have those things when we were young—so we *invented* them for *your* generation to enjoy. Now, arrogant young man, let me ask: what are *you* doing for the next generation?"

The applause from the audience surrounding them was resounding. The young man choked on his soft drink and did not utter another word.

Without a doubt, the secularist must sound equally haughty in the ears of God. He proclaims how intelligent he is and further insists upon the absolute correctness of the *truths* he has *discovered*. All the while he fails to give a single iota of consideration to the possibility that all of these things—his intelligence, the laws of the universe, the truths he has discovered, even his very existence—might *first* have been set in place by God Himself.

Although the secular worldview of Crowley, our atheist character from the first chapter, *seemed* to pack a devastating punch, as you will soon discover, his overconfidence will crumble into a heap when competently compared against *true truth*. Let us get right to it, shall we?

· 6 ·

THE STRAW MAN

*[They] changed the truth of God into a lie, and worshipped and served
the creature more than the Creator, who is blessed forever. Amen*
—Romans 1:25

The Magic Man in the sky/Mother Goose/tooth fairy scenario is an intimidating and often debilitating argument when deployed against unprepared Christians. The evolutionist, atheist, and agnostic are aware of its incapacitating muscle, and as a result, the scheme is frequently used in debate. The dishonesty of the argument, though, is that it is a *straw man*. As such, it need not be feared. It has no teeth. It is not the *genuine* argument.

THE CONVENIENT SCARECROW

A *straw man* is a fallacious argument based on a misrepresentation of the opponent's actual position. To *attack a straw man* is to create the illusion of having rebutted a proposition. This is done by replacing, in a sneaky manner, the actual position with a comparable, yet nonequivalent, suggestion: the *straw man*. Then, the covert *straw man* is refuted rather than the actual position itself.

The origins of the term *straw man* are unclear. One common explanation is that the concept may have originated with men who stood outside of courthouses, in ages past, each with a piece of straw discreetly tucked into his shoe, slightly exposed, to signify his willingness to be a false witness—in exchange for appropriate compensation.

Another more popular and more plausible possibility of the term's origin relates to humanlike figures manufactured out of straw. Reportedly, these straw men were used as dummies in military training, and other such endeavors, to represent the enemy. A straw dummy was easy to attack because it could not move, nor did it have the ability to fight back.

The *straw man technique* of debate is used in similar fashion and takes several recognizable forms, including:

- Presenting a distortion of the opponent's actual position on a matter and then refuting the misrepresented position. This gives the appearance that the opponent's actual position has been rebutted. This is what happened to Christopher in chapter 1. We will discuss that straw man in larger detail in the following pages.

- Quoting an opponent's words out of context. This is, in particular, a frustrating attack to defend because it first requires that the proper context be explained with compelling thoroughness. If one cannot convincingly explain the proper and original context, then his debate appears to crumble.

- Putting forth an example of a particular personality who insufficiently defends his position. That person is then presented as the ultimate defender of the position. Then, *that* person's arguments are refuted with ease, thus giving the appearance that every advocate of the position, and thus the position itself, has been surmounted.

- Inventing a fictitious, *like-minded* persona, expert, or group of experts who is then appealed to in the argument (e.g., "How can you not believe in evolution when *all the scientists* are in agreement that it is a proven fact?").

This last technique is one of the straw man arguments that Crowley used against Christopher. The atheist appealed to that supposed group of "all scientists" who agrees that evolution is settled truth. This claim can be easily refuted as an illustration of how a straw man works: While the vast majority of scientists do hold to a preponderance of today's evolution theory, stating that *all scientists* agree that evolution is the most satisfactory explanation for the existence of life is incorrect.

In reality, numerous reputable and distinguished scientists are on record to the contrary. They do not agree with many tenets of evolutionary thought. In addition, a reputable minority of scientists *within* the evolutionary community itself do not hold to the postulation that evolution is a *proven fact.* Therefore, this mystical academy of *all scientists* who believe evolution is proven fact is imaginary. It plainly does not exist.

But the secularist will try anything. Let us look back at the first technique we discussed: presenting a *distortion* of the opponent's actual position, and then refuting the distorted position. This often takes the form of oversimplifying or exaggerating an opponent's argument. For example:

> **Person A**: Our society should loosen the restrictions on gun ownership a bit. In so doing, our Second Amendment rights would be best served and protected.
>
> **Person B**: I can't believe you think that! Once our society has unrestricted access to guns, we will revert to the Wild West days!

Of course, Person A said nothing about *unrestricted* access to guns. In fact, he merely suggested that the current regulations be relaxed *a bit*. However, before he could explain what *a bit* meant, the argument was elevated and exaggerated to *unrestricted access*. Here's another example:

> **Person A:** Our society should be more judicious in its distribution of welfare funds. Vast numbers of people abuse the system without shame.
>
> **Person B:** I can't believe you would rob children of the ability to eat and to be educated. People like you would have millions of people starving in the street and children unable to read and write. You shouldn't be so stingy with government money.

The straw man is multifaceted in this example. Person A said nothing about taking food from needy children or depriving anyone of a decent education. Furthermore, the mention of *government money* was without consideration of the fact that the government *has* no money of its own. The money the government uses to distribute welfare funds comes from the taxes collected from its working citizens. Person A merely proposed that the process should be better scrutinized in order to keep the scammers from taking money from those who need it. However, Person

B was able to ratchet up the rhetoric to an emotional level that made Person A's argument seem unreasonable and untenable. He built a *straw man* and attacked *it* rather than dealing with the true issue at hand.

Crowley built several straw men scenarios against poor old Christopher. Once the straw men were constructed, he attacked those propositions as though they were the real subjects of the debate. The most devastating of his straw men he named "the Magic Man in the sky." As this book progresses, I will dismantle this straw man piece by piece. When I do, you will see that it is nothing to fear at all, just like the boogeyman a child only thinks is hiding in the bedroom closet, or the scarecrow strategically placed in a cornfield. The boogeyman is a frightening concept— but he does not exist. The scarecrow looks like a real man to the crow, and thus frightens it. Yet, in reality it is nothing more than a man's clothing stuffed with straw. It is as harmless as the boogeyman.

Let us now take a closer look at the secular boogeyman. We will take him apart piece by piece. It really is easier than you might think.

· 7 ·

DISMANTLING THE
STRAW MAN

S o, how is the straw man technique applicable to the Magic-
Man-in-the-sky scenario employed by our atheist friend
Crowley? His multifaceted attack against our Christian
student was an exaggeration as well as a blatant misrepresentation of Christopher's actual position. Crowley's use of the straw
man technique ratcheted up the conversation to a different
emotional level in order to avoid the actual debated topic: the

existence of God.

However, neither the Bible nor the knowledgeable Christian declares that God is magical or that He uses magic in His work. In fact, Scripture clearly *forbids* the use of magic or sorcery. How disingenuous are those who use the word *magic* to describe the unseen and frequently unexplainable works of God of which we Christians speak.

The evolutionist would be hard-pressed to defend the *magical* processes postulated in origins theory. How is life emerging from a random, unpurposed process that took place in a *primordial soup* (a mixture of organic compounds theorized to have given rise by *chance* to life on earth) not *magic*? This theoretical emergence of life has never been observed, nor has it ever been replicated. It is merely imagined. Is this not one manner in which *magic* defines itself—the mind *imagines* something that did not actually happen?

ABOUT THAT PRIMORDIAL SOUP ...

As mentioned in an earlier chapter, *abiogenesis*[1] (or *chemosynthesis*[2]) is the newer scientific term for the supposed spontaneous generation of life. *Spontaneous generation* is the supposed random, unpurposed emergence of life from previously nonliving matter and/or chemical compounds, over eons of time. According to this supposition, these bits of nonliving matter or chemical conglomerations, in the end, evolved into living, replicating, thinking, and creating beings.

In time, this process of turning nonliving materials and inorganic chemicals into living organisms is reported to have resulted in the multiplied millions of distinct and intricate species of life that now populate our planet. One of the biggest problems with this claim is that abiogenesis has not been scientifically demonstrated in the entirety of human existence. The proclaimed *truth* of abiogenesis is an immense scientific problem.

The most recent scientific experiments attempting to replicate abiogenesis have only been able to produce mere parts of the most elementary basic building blocks of life. None of these parts has ever exhibited anything close to *life*. Furthermore, even in those failed attempts at formulating life, human intervention and manipulation (intelligent input) were involved *by necessity*. An intelligent person in a lab applied measures of scientific manipulation. Yet, not a single *living* organism has ever been produced, not even in highly controlled laboratory situations. I would daresay that life would not generate from a haphazard and accidental primordial soup either. Yet, to this day, abiogenesis is the undeniable cornerstone of origins theory. Sounds like a purely magical process; would you not agree?

Consider the following declaration from a decidedly evolution-based college science textbook, published in 2003. The book's author, Dr. James D. Mauseth, professor of integrative biology at the University of Texas, made this categorical pronouncement: "The most seriously considered hypothesis about the origins of life is chemosynthesis."[3]

According to Dr. Mauseth, there is not much room for debate on this point. Yet his explanation of life's origins depends on processes that are unknown, unseen, and undemonstrated. Hmm . . . Sounds like *magic* to me.

ABRACADABRA!

The evolution community has recently hailed the aforementioned attempts at the manipulated production of the rudimentary components of life as proof positive that life could have originated by mere spontaneity. Conveniently, they claim that the process would just have to be given enough *time* and just the right set of *circumstances* to actually work. (Wink, wink). In truth, these experiments prove no such thing.

The statistical chances are next to nil that nonliving matter or a hodgepodge assortment of chemicals, minding its own business, could have arranged itself into a simple, single-celled living organism. The probabilities of this occurrence are beyond the bounds of reasonable and logical mathematical comprehension.

Consider this illustration. My computer could never arbitrarily write the four billion-byte program code that is enclosed within a single DNA molecule, no matter how much time was allotted its attempts. Could it happen in a year? Could the computer write the necessary program in a *thousand* years? Would the program come into existence after *millions* or *billions* of years? The math says *no*. Even if the program did mystically arise, we nevertheless have to consider that the computer program, as marvelous as it would be, still does not approximate the complexity of a single living organism—much less millions and millions of different living organisms.

To further complicate the equation, one has to ponder other significant and relatable questions. From where did the computer originate in the first place? Who programs it? How does it initiate the random process of writing the code? Where does the intelligent code within the computer originate? Where does the energy come from that is required for the computer to operate?

Indeed, what determines the specific coding equations and patterns that operate, with preciseness, to *create* anything? Why would the computer *want* to randomly generate a code for life? And *how* could it want to generate a code for life?

When these and other corresponding elements factor in, the possibility of the random generation of DNA code for even a single molecule becomes impossible—in staggering proportions.

I find it unfathomable by any reasonable stretch of the imagination to believe that an unplanned and uninitiated (devoid of intelligent input) primordial soup could have birthed itself and then written the code for life, even with billions of years to do so. I must apologize for not having enough faith to believe that it *could* or *would*. It appears the evolutionist possesses much more overwhelming faith in this matter than I.

A MAGIC MAN IN THE MUD?

However, if one truly wishes to speak of *magical processes*, consider the scenario related to origins theory and evolution. Does not evolution postulation demand that we believe in a mystical (unobserved, undemonstrated, and unknowable) process wherein *magic* mud in a magical but nonliving primordial pond developed magical soup which magically gave rise to magical living molecules (only once) that magically decided to self-replicate over magical periods of eons of time with magical inputs of outside sources of mystical power? Moreover—what accounts for these mystical and magical organisms *deciding* to branch off into other magical living organisms until many millions of intricately different living organisms, each with multiple and interdependent systems, came into being? Additionally—what accounts for the fact that some of these organisms eventually evolved into human beings who now have the capacity to *think* of evolution theory? Phew! Talk about magic! Again, the *magical* process of evolution, devoid of any intelligent input, demands much more faith than I am capable of imagining or expressing.

Although chemists Stanley Miller and Harold Urey[4] did form simple amino acids (the basic building blocks for life) in their experiments in 1952, all of them lacked *chirality* (pronounced kī-RA-la-tee); that is, molecular *handedness*. This fact is of paramount importance. Let me explain.

A handshake illustrates the concept of *handedness* or *chirality*. You reach out with your right hand. The other person extends his right hand to you. The two hands are mirror images of each other, and they fit together perfectly as they intertwine to form the handclasp. Similarly, to work properly, molecules must have a precise *fit* regarding their chemical properties. If the chemical properties do not fit—or possess chirality (handedness)—they do not work. Chirality is essential for molecules to function.

Although two chemical molecules may seem to have the same elements with compatible properties, they can still have different structures or handedness. On the other hand, when two molecules appear identical and their structures differ only by being mirror images of each other, those molecules are declared to have *chirality*. Chirality provides the unique shape for proteins and DNA. Without it, the biochemical processes in our bodies could not function. Stated simply, *without chirality, we cannot have life.* Since the Miller-Urey experiments failed to produce molecules with chirality, they failed to create real *life.*

"It is a universally accepted fact of chemistry that chirality cannot be created in chemical molecules by a random process," says Dr. Charles McCombs, an organic chemist who holds twenty chemical patents. "The fact that chirality was missing in those amino acids (Miller-Urey) is not just a problem to be debated, it points to a catastrophic failure that 'life' cannot come from chemicals by natural processes."[5]

Much about our world is still not completely understood. From the atomic world to the microbial world, we are consistently discovering a great deal of new information. From the jungles, to the depths of the oceans, to the farthest reaches of the universe— an immense quantity of wonders continues to exist.

The total estimated number of species on the face of the earth today ranges from 2 million to more than 200 million, depending on who is doing the estimating and how the word *species* is defined. Regardless, we frequently discover new species of life. Are the unknown, unseen, undiscovered, and unexplained elements of life and the forces of nature and its laws relegated to mere *magic*—only because the scientist has yet to discover or explain them? Obviously, they are not. Nevertheless, the antagonist of Christianity wishes to describe the unknown forces and elements of the *Creator*, the God of the Bible, as mere magic. Again, this straw man is forced to depend upon deception and hypocrisy.

There are several more examples of "magical" considerations within the realm of science. Consider the unfathomable depths of quantum physics. Quantum science is the study of the smallest particles known to man. A little over a century ago, we discovered that the atom, previously thought to be the smallest particle known to man, was made up of still smaller particles. Now we understand that those smaller particles are made up of even smaller particles, or waves and electromagnetic forces. The deeper we look, astonishingly, the more we find—even in the unseen world of *quanta particles*.

We now understand that the way these tiny elements interact appears to be outside every boundary of the known physical laws of the universe. Yet, these particles, acting without reliable prediction, in the final analysis serve to make up everything known to man. This knowledge includes the laws by which we govern our lives and by which we build several of our existing technologies. For example, lasers, MRI machines, and computer equipment originate from our still-limited understanding of quantum mechanics.

Would a true scientist describe quantum theory as *magic* merely because there is much about quantum mechanics that is still unobserved, unexplained, and, for all practical purposes, unknowable? I would think not. Likewise, neither the Bible nor the knowledgeable Christian uses this term to describe the creative works of God. Its use is reserved for the biblical antagonist, who seeks to discredit the argument for God's existence by employing a straw man from the *opening of the debate.*

A MERE MAN?

The exposure of our *straw man* does not end with the word *magic*. It continues with the word *man,* as used in the phrase *the magic man in the sky.* Again, neither the Bible nor the studied Christian speaks of God as a mere *man.* True, Scripture says that Jesus Christ *became* a man—known as the Incarnation. However, remember, God *put on* human likeness and appeared in human form in the person of Jesus Christ. Why did God, the Creator, *put on* human form? Specifically—because He is *not* a mere man. God is the definitive reality. Humanity is but one of His marvelous creations. God is *other* than and bigger than a mere man.

Consider the following scriptural truths about God and the necessity of the Incarnation:

> And also the Strength of Israel will not lie nor repent: for he is not a man that he should repent. (1 Samuel 15:29)

> For he is not a man, as I am, that I should answer him, and we should come together in judgment. (Job 9:32)

> [Jesus] is the image of the invisible God, the firstborn of every creature. (Colossians 1:15)

> [Jesus,] being in the form of God, thought it not robbery to be equal with God: but made himself of no reputation, and took upon him the form of a servant, and was made in the likeness of men. (Philippians 2:6–7)

However, the Bible also declares that we are made in God's *image.* Would not that declaration argue for the fact that God is like a man since we are made like Him? I will concede that if one did not understand the entire biblical concept of the representation of God in His reality, he or she could be confused by this biblical declaration: "God created man in his own image, in the image of God created he him; male and female created he them." (Genesis 1:27)

The answer lies in understanding the meaning of the Hebrew word used in the original text. The Hebrew word translated "image" is *tselem.* This word, in its contextual sense, means a *resemblance* or a *representative figure.* It does not mean a *carbon copy of* or a *smaller version of* something. The idea portrayed in the word is that man is the crowning glory of all of God's creation. The idea of the unique creation of man and woman came from the mind and heart of God.

Humankind was to be different from anything else He fashioned. Every other living thing God created would live and act in accordance with an instinctive nature. However, humans would be special. We would have *choice.* We could think, plan, design, and create. We would be able to speak, to write, to pass on generational knowledge, and to commune with our Creator. No other living creature would ever be able to do these things with such magnanimous splendor. This gift was reserved only for humankind.

Since God Himself can create, design, think, communicate, pass along generational knowledge, and speak with an intricate language—and *we* can—it is in this way that we were made in God's *image (tselem).* Compared to all other living things, the human race is unequaled. We are a *universe* apart from the next most intelligent living being on earth.

The majority of scientists agree the most intelligent animal next to man is the chimpanzee. Chimps are marvelous and fascinating creatures, to be sure. However, chimps, to this day, swing in trees, eat bananas, pick each other's fleas, and sling poo. They always have, and they always will.

Man, on the other hand, has explored the depths of the oceans, the heights of the heavens, and the depths of the quantum world. Our race *alone* has planted a flag on the moon. We have launched probes into deep space. We fly through the air in vehicles that we first imagined, then designed, created, and now pilot. It is humans who sail the oceans and navigate highways. We invent and build intricate technologies, erect libraries, manufacture computers, and share our ideas with people on the other side of the world.

Chimpanzees are . . . well . . . *chimpanzees.* They do what chimps have always done. They do not come close to the universe of man's intelligence. Nothing does in all of creation, except God Himself—who is another unfathomable number of universe-steps away from man. Of all the things God created, only man is made in God's *image.* This biblical understanding in no way suggests that God is merely a larger or more intelligent form of a man.

In his use of the phrase *magic man,* the atheist is disingenuously reducing God the Creator to a mere human. The technique conjures up the image of an old, incompetent, perhaps slightly larger mortal waving a magic wand over his minions on the earth. The use of this straw man tactic reduces the concept of God to a simplistic caricature. This is often its intended purpose.

Nevertheless, let us not forget that the atheist, Crowley, also expressed something about our magic man living *in the sky.* In the next chapter, we will put a match to that part of the bale of straw as well.

· 8 ·

LOOKING DOWN FROM
ON HIGH

Alas, the straw man presentation of the "magic man in the sky" does not end with what we have already discussed. Once more, a term sneaks into the argument that we Christians do not employ in our speech nor embrace in our biblical understanding of the truth about God. Neither the Bible nor the one familiar with it believes that God lives in the *sky*.

In fairness, perhaps the antagonist means to speak of heaven when he uses the word *sky*. However, the atheist's purposed use of the term *sky* invokes an image of a man with a magic wand, floating around just about the level of the clouds, performing silly and manipulative magic. Once the concept of *God in heaven* is reduced to this silly caricature, half of our rival's battle is won. If this indeed is what Christians believe about who God is, how He works, and where He exists in His ultimate reality, well then, we should all be consigned to a mental facility. Again, I believe this is precisely what the *magic man in the sky* postulation intends to suggest, that not only do we hold to this belief, but that we are maniacal from the outset and incapable of an enlightened debate.

To be fair about this matter, the Bible and the Christian do frequently speak of *heaven*. Moreover, on occasion, we refer to it as being *up there*. The doctrine of heaven is too lengthy to expound in its entirety in this chapter, but to encapsulate the biblical understanding of heaven, let us state that heaven is simply the exclusive realm and domain of God—and it is not *in the sky*. The Bible is clear on this matter.

In reality, heaven describes the *dimension* where God dwells rather than another level or height in the heavens. The following chapter will rationally clarify this declaration.

The Bible frequently uses the word *sky*, but it does not refer to it as being the dwelling place of God. If the Bible even comes close to saying that, it is in a poetic or symbolic sense and not in a literal one. Those who do not know the Bible would not know this. They use only the terms they know.

Heaven describes God's dwelling place. The use of this word, in context, does not mean *the heavens* or the abode of the planets and galaxies, but rather, another dimension, or plane of existence, reserved for God and His heavenly creation.

The biblical Hebrew mind expressed the concept of the heavens in three distinct ways. One use of the word *heavens* meant the sky or the atmospheric portion of our earth's realm of existence. Thus, the birds are said to take flight "in the heavens."

Another understanding of the heavens is as being *beyond* the skies and the atmosphere, to include the realm of the stars and planets, the sun and the moon, and beyond even them. Thus, the Bible also speaks of the heavens as being the place of the heavenly bodies. These first two concepts of the *heavens* are portrayed in the Bible as mere creations of God. The Creator Himself is above even these realms of heaven.

Finally, the Bible speaks of a *third heaven*. The use of the word *heaven* in this sense is reserved for the special and unique home of God Himself. It is neither the sky nor the domain of the stars and planets. Rather, it is the dimension in which God dwells. Following are a few scriptures that confirm these truths:

> O LORD our Lord, how excellent is thy name in all the earth! who hast set thy glory *above the heavens*. Out of the mouth of babes and sucklings hast thou ordained strength because of thine enemies, that thou mightest still the enemy and the avenger. When I consider *thy heavens*, the work of thy fingers, the moon and the stars, which thou hast ordained; what is man, that thou art mindful of him? and the son of man, that thou visitest him? For thou hast made him a little lower than the angels, and hast crowned him with glory and honour. Thou madest him to have dominion over the works of thy hands; thou hast put all things under his feet: all sheep and oxen, yea, and the beasts of the field, the fowl of the air, and the fish of the sea, and whatsoever passeth through the paths of the seas. O LORD our Lord, how excellent is thy name in all the earth! (Psalm 8:1–9; emphasis added)

> I knew a man in Christ about fourteen years ago, (whether in the body, I cannot tell; or whether out of the body, I cannot tell: God knoweth;) such an one caught up to the third heaven. And I knew such a man, (whether in the body, or out

of the body, I cannot tell: God knoweth;) how that he was caught up into paradise, and heard unspeakable words, which it is not lawful for a man to utter. (2 Corinthians 12:2–4)

On occasion, the Scripture declares that God is *looking down* from heaven—*upon* us. However, do we not also look down upon the microbial world as we observe it through a microscope? Yet, clearly, we are not dwelling *in the sky* or literally *above* the microbes (perhaps some of those same microbes can also be found on the ceiling *above* us or on a shelf *behind* us), but rather, we observe them from another dimension of reality. They are within our world, and we, at the same time, are within their world of existence. Yet, we view them and manipulate the conditions of their world and existence, and all the while, they have no idea of our existence. When we observe the microbes through the lens of a microscope, we are in a position of *looking down* upon them, from *above,* but in reality, we dwell *among* them, and they among us. While we peer at their world and their humble existence through a microscope lens, we are merely in a physical position defined as *looking down.*

More than likely, something similar is meant when the Scripture declares that God *looks down* upon us from *heaven* (for example, Psalm 33:13; 53:2).

THE STRAW MAN HAS NO CLOTHING!

Thus, the Magic (straw) Man in the sky is exposed. The ridiculous, three-pronged attack that seeks to reduce the biblical position to a trite and vain argument has been dismantled.

So if God is not some mystical, magic man in the sky—that only a child would believe in, but not something a refined, educated, and enlightened individual would consider—then who is He, and how do we refer to Him and His existence? Again, the complete answer to that question would fill another book. Therefore, I will give a synopsis of the contextual and biblical understanding that answers the question.

God is *other* than us. He is the ultimate reality. We are simply one of the many marvelous things He made. Think of it this way: an ornate table produced in a carpenter's shop is, in fact, a solid reality; however, the ultimate reality is the carpenter himself. Without the carpenter, the table could not exist. Both the table and the carpenter are real, but the carpenter is the *ultimate* reality. The table reflects much about the carpenter. Its visible qualities reveal something about the artisan's eye for detail, beauty, and design. However, to only see the table does not even come close to knowing the carpenter who manufactured it. The artisan, in an indescribable way, is *other than* the table.

That is how it is with God. His creation, and even man himself, is glorious. By observing what He created, we can understand much about the Creator. We can discern that He is intelligent beyond our comprehension, and that He has an eye for beauty, detail, and order beyond our meager understanding. We can also discern something of His unthinkable power and majesty. We can identify enough about Him to know that He exists, and that we did not arrive here through mere random generation or through an undirected, unguided, naturalistic process. We can recognize enough about God to be *without excuse* before our Creator.

Still, with all this knowledge, we cannot comprehend God in a complete fashion, any more than we could fully comprehend the maker of a table only by observing the table.

CONSIDER THE FOLLOWING PASSAGES:

That which may be known of God is manifest in [men]; for God hath shewed it unto them. For the invisible things of him from the creation of the world are clearly seen, being understood by the things that are made, even his eternal power and Godhead; so that they are *without excuse*: Because that, when they knew God, they glorified him not as God, neither were thankful; but became vain in their imaginations, and their foolish heart was darkened. Professing themselves to be wise, they became fools. (Romans 1:19–22; emphasis added)

God is outright and without qualification—*other* than we are. God lovingly chose to take on the form of a man and step into our dimension of reality that we might know Him in a more intimate manner. When He did that, we discovered something about Him that we could not have known otherwise. We discovered the depths of His sacrificial love and the special place that we of the human species hold in His heart. We learned that He laid down His earthly existence, within His perfect plan, even unto a brutal and unthinkable death that we might have life with Him—forever.

[God] hath delivered us from the power of darkness, and hath translated us into the kingdom of his dear Son: in whom we have redemption through his blood, even the forgiveness of sins: who is the *image of the invisible God*, the firstborn of every creature. (Colossians 1:13–15; emphasis added)

God, who at sundry times and in divers manners spake in time past unto the fathers by the prophets, hath in these last days *spoken unto us by his Son*, whom he hath appointed heir of all things, by whom also he made the worlds; who being the brightness of his glory, and the *express image of his person*, and upholding all things by the word of his power . . . (Hebrews 1:1–3; emphasis added).

Where does God dwell? Without doubt, He does not reside in the sky. He dwells within His own glory—in another dimension that is as real as ours yet, at the same time, is unseen by us. That dimension, or reality, for the sake of simplicity, is called *heaven* in His Word.

One might ask, how can something be unseen and yet an absolute and solid reality at the same time? Read on…

· 9 ·

THE SEEN AND THE UNSEEN

Things which are seen were not made of things which do appear.
—Hebrews 11:3

The following information is reproduced from a startling article in the June 2005 issue of *Discover* magazine. It was written by Tim Folger, and the topic is *quantum theory*. The provocative title of the article is: "If an Electron Can Be in Two Places at Once, Why Can't You?"

Take your time and thoughtfully read the words. They contain a brief synopsis of what recent scientific discovery has disclosed regarding the unseen forces that determine how you and I live our lives. Most secular scientists will fail to see the biblical and spiritual significance of these discoveries—I trust you will see them.

"About 80 years ago, scientists discovered that it is possible to be in two locations at the same time—at least for an atom or a subatomic particle, such as an electron. For such tiny objects, the world is governed by a madhouse set of physical laws known as quantum mechanics. At that size range, every bit of matter and energy exists in a state of blurry flux, allowing it to occupy not just two locations but also an infinite number of them simultaneously. The world we see follows a totally different set of rules, of course.

What nobody can explain is why the universe seems split into these two separate and irreconcilable realities. If everything in the universe is made of quantum things, why don't we see quantum effects in everyday life? . . . Many physicists find this issue so vexing that they ignore it entirely. Instead, they focus on what does work about their theories. The equations of quantum mechanics do a fantastic job describing the behavior of particles in an atom smasher, the nuclear reactions that make the sunshine, and the chemical processes that underlie biology.

The maddening part of the problem is that the ability of particles to exist in two places at once is not a mere theoretical abstraction. It is a very real aspect of how the subatomic world works, and it has been experimentally confirmed many times over."[1]

Science seems to be confirming what students of the Bible have been contemplating for thousands of years. Most scientists had previously relegated these considerations to the realm of esoterical ponderings and spiritual mysticism. Now we are beginning to discover how certain long-held biblical truths may possess scientific and weighty evidence of certainty. Based on the afore-mentioned scientific verifications, you can now better understand:

1. God's ability to be both real, in the physical sense, and yet unseen.

2. God's ability to be in one place or multiple places or even *every place* all at once.

3. How two or more realities can exist side by side, yet one or more of these realities does not have the ability to see the other realities.

4. How God, operating in the earthly realm in the person of Jesus, could manipulate or use certain quantum principles and laws to work what we would observe and classify as *miracles*. Our Creator of these quantum principles would not have a problem, for example, calming the waves with a command or healing a sick person as though he had not been sick. He could raise a man from the dead as though he had not died, walk through a wall into a locked room, or even *rise from a grave* and present Himself alive again.

Consider also that we are only scratching the surface concerning our understanding of quantum mechanics. This field of study is one of the most fascinating scientific reinforcements of the biblical faith and certain astonishing declarations revealed within the pages of the Word of God.

Take a moment and ponder the following passages of scripture in light of the *Discover* article on quantum mechanics:

For which cause we faint not; but though our outward man perish, yet the inward man is renewed day by day. For our light affliction, which is but for a moment, worketh for us a far more exceeding and eternal weight of glory; while we look not at the things which are seen, but at the things which are not seen: for the things which are seen are temporal; but the things which are not seen are eternal. (2 Corinthians 4:16–18)

Now faith is the substance of things hoped for, the evidence of things not seen. For by it the elders obtained a good report. Through faith we understand that the worlds were framed by the word of God, so that things which are seen were not made of things which do appear. (Hebrews 11:1–3)

No man hath seen God at any time. If we love one another, God dwelleth in us, and his love is perfected in us. Hereby know we that we dwell in him, and he in us, because he hath given us of his Spirit. And we have seen and do testify that the Father sent the Son to be the Saviour of the world. (1 John 4:12–14)

After this I looked, and, behold, a door was opened in heaven: and the first voice which I heard was as it were of a trumpet talking with me; which said, Come up hither, and I will shew thee things which must be hereafter. And immediately I was in the spirit: and, behold, a throne was set in heaven, and one sat on the throne. (Revelation 4:1–2)

Each of these passages is about two thousand years old. With the latest discoveries in the field of quantum science, these biblical declarations do not seem so odd or esoterical anymore, do they? Now these assertions have scientific credence that underscores and highlights their plausibility.

This is not to suggest that our discoveries in quantum mechanics are the *definitive answers* to certain biblical mysteries, nor am I suggesting that God relegates His working and miraculous interventions solely through the principles of quantum mechanics. In fact, I am not indicating that God works through the principles of quantum mechanics *at all*. These examples of current scientific knowledge are only offered to demonstrate how certain biblical principles that were previously relegated to the realm of the *spiritual* and *magical* workings of God *do* have real scientific counterparts. No longer can a secularist categorically dismiss the claims of the Bible as being scientific impossibilities. We now have illustrations from quantum scientific truths which indicate that certain biblical claims *are* scientific and verified possibilities.

Certainly, a born-again believer does not need the evidence of quantum mechanics or any other scientific evidence to trust the Word of God. However, God has done a wonderful and gracious thing by peeling back the skin of a few of His wondrous creations so we may obtain a glimpse of the glorious possibilities of how it all might fit together.

This leads us to a brief discourse on the *supernatural*. What do we mean when we use the word *supernatural*? The evolutionist and the atheist do not care for the word. To an unbeliever, the word denotes something otherworldly or imaginary. Critics define the term as something that is beyond the realm of science and reality. Supernatural, to them, typically invokes the idea that something is *make-believe*.

However, in its most common rendering, supernatural is defined as simply "relating to an order of existence beyond the visible observable universe."[2] Thus, the term commonly relates to the spiritual realm or the things of God or of gods.

The word *super* means *over and above* or of *uncommon strength or characteristic*. The word *natural* means *having to do with the realm of the seen and understood*. It would seem, then, that the word *supernatural* could also be defined as *over and above what we can see or understand in the natural realm in which we exist*. Remarkably, this definition of supernatural perfectly describes the realm of reality that the Bible represents as being the domain of God.

However, the word *supernatural* also describes, for instance, the realm of quantum mechanics. The totality of the world of quanta is over and above anything we can see or comprehend with certainty within the natural world in which we live. Reconsider this excerpt, previously quoted from the *Discover* article we just read: "The world we see totally follows a different set of rules, of course."

Our realm of existence is the *world we see*—it is the natural. The quanta world is another realm of reality, and it operates by a different set of rules. Hence, it is *supernatural*. It is *other than* or *over and above* the natural world.

We cannot see the quanta particles, waves, and energy forces in a *natural* way. Nor can we yet, to this day, understand the totality of the interaction of these particles, waves, and forces upon our world and our lives. Yet, we understand that they *do* interact with us, and in fact, they make up the stuff of life itself. If these unseen and incomprehensible particles did not exist, *we* would not exist.

Therefore, when the Bible-believing Christian speaks of the *supernatural* nature of God or the unseen world of His domain and His invisible and incomprehensible power and glory, we have not lost our minds, nor are we operating in a childish understanding of a *Magic Man in the sky*. To the contrary, when we use the word *supernatural,* we are merely attesting to the known and scientific fact that we encounter forces and realities beyond our world and our current understanding.

Why is this factual concept so difficult for the secularist to grasp? If he were truly "scientific," he would have no problem acknowledging that forces and realities beyond his limited knowledge *do* exist.

In the next chapter, we will examine an irrefutable illustration of how two realities may subsist side by side with one reality being completely unaware that the other reality exists. In other words, I will explain the *supernatural* in a very *naturalistic* way.

If you are a secularist, you may not wish to read any further—unless you are prepared to have your world shoved around a bit.

· 10 ·

THE TALE OF
TWO DIMENSIONS

L et us now consider a practical and easily understood idea. The illustration displays how something can be seen and unseen, at the same time. Is it actually possible that a solid, flesh-and-blood reality can be in the presence of and surrounded by another flesh-and-blood reality, yet one of those realities is totally unaware of the other? Yes.

Imagine with me for a moment that you are looking at a five-thousand-acre prairie ranch. In the middle of it all, in the farm's rolling backcountry, you see a five-acre pond. Under the surface of that pond is a complete ecosystem—another world, if you will.

Everything necessary for sustaining the life of a fish is provided, not only from within that watery environment, but from *outside* of it as well. Yet, the fish is totally unaware of the necessity or existence of such provisions. I am speaking of at least the sun, the rain, and the oxygen of the atmosphere that surrounds and intersects with the pond. The pond is also affected by *dangerous* outside and unseen elements as well, such as fertilizers, poisons, air pollution, chemicals, and garbage.

Living within his world of reality, Mr. Fish is flesh and blood. He is as real as we are. Granted, he is a different sort of reality and a different type of flesh, yet we cannot deny that the fish is real. Everything within his world is *reality*, and it is physical, from beginning to end.

Much of his world is incomprehensible to him. A fish has no inkling of the photosynthesis process that takes place every day within his pond. Nor does he understand the delicate chemical balances necessary to sustain his life. He experiences, perhaps with dread, that something is wrong when the balances are sometimes disturbed. However, the fish's understanding of such things is a universe removed from his capability to comprehend them as we do.

Within the world of our Mr. Fish, he communicates, eats, mates, plays, and survives. In other words, he goes about the stuff of his life until he dies. He participates in his life's journey within *his* realm of reality. He cannot live outside that realm. He cannot *see* outside that realm, other than a glimpse of shadowy figures just above the surface of his reality—and this is only from time to time. When he gets these occasional glimpses from above, he does not have a clue what he is seeing. His life in the pond is regularly affected by chemical reactions, unseen forces, and indistinct figures of living things from another world, all of which he has no ability to comprehend.

Astonishingly but true, Mr. Fish has no understandable idea of the rest of the world around him. The totality of his existence is below the surface of a five-acre pond on a stretch of undeveloped land in the middle of a five-thousand-acre ranch. He has no notions about human life, cities, or the two million species of other life forms all around him, no concept of interstate highways, governments, politics, wars, airplane flight, space travel, or the heavenly bodies of the universe. What a lucky fish, for the most part!

He cannot fathom mathematics, scientific exploration, and cultivation of food sources, factories, or communication technologies. A computer, a library, or a book would be meaningless to Mr. Fish. In fact, he cannot fathom that you are reading about his existence at this moment.

He has no ability to comprehend what lies outside the boundaries of our own solar system and beyond that into deep space. In fact, he does not comprehend what a solar system *is* or that one exists. None of these concepts has ever crossed his mind. Moreover, he is satisfied, to the point of perfection, with his lack of knowledge and understanding. He is convinced that the sum total of reality exists below the surface of the pond. It is his entire world, his universe. However, he is entirely wrong in his limited assessment of what is *real* and what is not.

Now consider this: We can enter the fish's world, but it cannot enter ours. Fish are not equipped to live in our world, but we can be equipped to live both in ours and in theirs. We can don scuba equipment and *appear* in their world. However, even if they notice us there, they have not a clue as to what they are seeing. They may see our forms, but they do not comprehend us as we are. They might think they know something about us. However, in truth, they know precious little about us.

Think of it: Two flesh-and-blood realities existing side by side. One is inside of and exists within the realm of the other. Yet the one just below the water's surface has no idea of the depth to which the other reality exists. In fact, the fish would be overwhelmed if it could somehow discover and experience the reality that has existed all about him—all along.

If Mr. Fish had the ability, he might insist to the other fish that such a reality does not and could not exist because he cannot see it and fathom it. Nothing in his reality suggests that another *world* exists all around him. However, he would be wrong—eternally wrong. There *is* another dimension of unseen reality.

This illustrative scenario is comparable to the situation of the evolutionist/atheist. He is living in his fishpond. In the midst of it, he declares with limited knowledge that he has his world all figured out. At the same time, he denies the slightest possibility that other powers, forces, and realities may exist just outside of his reality—just through the surface of this thing we call *life*. The evolutionist will categorically declare that "the evidence is in—evolution is proven, scientific fact, and creationists have been proven wrong by science."

The atheist proclaims, "You cannot prove the existence of God. You cannot see Him nor can you naturalistically explain Him. He is merely your magic man in the sky. Therefore, He does not exist."

These two typical representatives of the secular worldview sound just as condescending as would our Mr. Fish if he were to make the following proclamations from within his universe of reality.

THE ENLIGHTENED SPEECH OF DR. DAWFINS

Fellow fish, a number of citizens among us have recently spoken of unseen forces, powers, and even living beings that they claim to have gotten glimpses of over the many years of our world's existence. Some claim that these beings have a sort of sway over *our* very being. How ridiculous!

Yes, we have all experienced unexplained phenomena on occasion. But I propose to you that all of these can be elucidated with natural, reasonable common sense, and scientific explanations. There is no need to believe in a magic fish in the sky. We all know that our world ends just above us.

Those who have tried to penetrate the barrier above us either have seen nothing but blurriness or have not returned to us at all. To suggest there is anything more powerful outside of our world that has any fishy presence or power to it at all is . . . well . . . ridiculous.

Let us, therefore, hush all this nonsense of another life outside our world. Let us silence the stupidity of the superstitious among us who claim that other forms of life and superior or even supernatural beings exist in some imaginary, unseen, and magical world. Let us deal with what we know, what we can see, and what we can explain. This is the logical and enlightened way to live at peace with one another within our world.

Does this resounding denial of *anything* supernatural sound familiar?

Now that you understand that it is possible, without question, for two worlds of flesh-and-blood reality to exist side by side, and even within each other's reality, yet with one incapable of comprehending the other, consider these scriptures:

[We] have renounced the hidden things of dishonesty, not walking in craftiness, nor handling the word of God deceitfully; but by manifestation of the truth commending ourselves to every man's conscience in the sight of God. But if our gospel be hid, it is hid to them that are lost: in whom the god of *this world* hath blinded the minds of them which believe not, lest the light of the glorious gospel of Christ, who is the image of God, should shine unto them. (2 Corinthians 4:2–4; emphasis added)

I the Lord have called thee in righteousness, and will hold thine hand, and will keep thee, and give thee for a covenant of the people, for a light of the Gentiles; To open the blind eyes, to bring out the prisoners from the prison, and them that sit in darkness out of the prison house. (Isaiah 42:6–7)

And Jesus said, For judgment I am come into this world, that they which see not might see; and that they which see might be made blind. (John 9:39)

[Stephen], being full of the Holy Ghost, looked up stedfastly into heaven, and saw the glory of God, and Jesus standing on the right hand of God, and said, Behold, I see the heavens opened, and the Son of man standing on the right hand of God. Then they cried out with a loud voice, and stopped their ears, and ran upon him with one accord . . . (Acts 7:55–57)

It is written, Eye hath not seen, nor ear heard, neither have entered into the heart of man, the things which God hath prepared for them that love him. But God hath revealed them unto us by his Spirit: for the Spirit searcheth all things, yea, the deep things of God. (1 Corinthians 2:9–10)

Consider again our new understanding of quantum particles and the unseen realities of the quantum world. That world is real, and it is verified by science. It is pulsating with forces and laws that govern our universe of reality. Consider also our new understanding of Mr. Fish and his closed-in yet *real* world. When keeping these scientific realities and the preceding logical illustration in mind, numerous scriptural truths take on a completely new depth of understanding.

A COUPLE MORE EXAMPLES

Before this chapter of thought is closed, consider a few more examples that are comparable to the pond story. I am convinced God has provided them to ensure that we are *without excuse*.

If the fishpond illustration was a revelation, consider the anthill. It is similar to the fishpond, in that it is filled with life, yet it does not exist in a *watery* reality. Instead, it exists in the same reality, atmosphere, and world in which we humans exist. Yet the ants, like the fish, are also unaware of our existence and all of the other things of this world that were mentioned in the fishpond illustration. Yet, they all exist. They are physical realities. To the ant, they would be *supernatural*.

Now consider this scenario for a moment. What if, when the ant died, it could somehow be transformed into a new creature? What if, upon leaving its world, it could become a human? If that could happen, then in an instant, the ant would be aware of its surroundings in the same way that we are aware of ours. The ant would be speechless and overwhelmed when, having become a man, he finds himself standing beside his old anthill of existence.

Having left the pile of dirt below him that he thought was the sum total of his life, he would quickly discover that an entire universe of reality exists all about him. He never saw it before now—but there it is! *It was around him all along!*

This new world of existence that the ant/man is now experiencing, and the universe in which it is contained, goes on forever.

It has no end, especially considering from where he just came. He now begins to weep, realizing that the pile of dirt he cherished while he lived in it was but a shadow of the reality that existed all around him.

Does this scenario sound familiar at all? Does this not sound like the memorable passages of scripture describing the entry into our new life upon exiting this world? Does the Bible not speak of a new existence—a new life that does not end—without death, without pain? Does it not speak of the old things passing away and the new things now being among us? In fact, the Bible declares all of these things. Consider the following examples:

> For what is a man profited, if he shall gain the whole world, and lose his own soul? or what shall a man give in exchange for his soul? For the Son of man shall come in the glory of his Father with his angels; and then he shall reward every man according to his works. Verily I say unto you, There be some standing here, which shall not taste of death, till they see the Son of man coming in his kingdom. (Matthew 16:26–28)

> And I heard a great voice out of heaven saying, Behold, the tabernacle of God is with men, and he will dwell with them, and they shall be his people, and God himself shall be with them, and be their God. And God shall wipe away all tears from their eyes; and there shall be no more death, neither sorrow, nor crying, neither shall there be any more pain: for the former things are passed away. And he that sat upon the throne said, Behold, I make all things new. And he said unto me, Write: for these words are true and faithful. (Revelation 21:3–5)

> For we that are in this tabernacle [body] do groan, being burdened: not for that we would be unclothed, but clothed upon, that mortality might be swallowed up of life. (2 Corinthians 5:4)

But some man will say, How are the dead raised up? and with what body do they come? Thou fool, that which thou sowest is not quickened, except it die . . . So also is the resurrection of the dead. It is sown in corruption; it is raised in incorruption: it is sown in dishonour; it is raised in glory: it is sown in weakness; it is raised in power: it is sown a natural body; it is raised a spiritual [supernatural] body. There is a natural body, and there is a spiritual [supernatural] body. (1 Corinthians 15:35–36, 42–44)

Again, with your new understanding, these scriptures are, without a doubt, more meaningful to you now. You have nothing to fear by believing the Word of God as absolute truth. It has stood the test of time. Now, as you have seen, it also stands the test of scientific plausibility. Furthermore, it stands the test of logical and illustrative plausibility.

Before we leave this train of thought, consider one more brief illustration. Let us think about the microbial world that we mentioned in chapter 8.

SAY HELLO TO MY LITTLE FRIEND...

The microbial world is yet another reality. This world exists at the infinitesimal level. It is unseen to us by our naked eyes, and our world is unseen and incomprehensible to microbes. Yet, we may peer *down* at them. And remember from chapter 8 that it is only because of the *position* of our eyes as we use a microscope that we are looking *down upon them.*

In reality, we exist in their world, and they exist throughout ours. Yet one reality exists without knowledge of the other. The illustrations of this truth are almost limitless. I am certain that you could now think of many more on your own. These examples from life serve to show us the realities of the supernatural. They also demonstrate, with great plausibility, the realities of the domain, power, and glory of God Himself. These illustrations and the quantum world of science, I am convinced, have been revealed to us in these last days in order that we are, again, without excuse.

> For the wrath of God is revealed from heaven against all ungodliness and unrighteousness of men, who hold the truth in unrighteousness; because that which may be known of God is manifest in them; for God hath shewed it unto them. For the invisible things of him from the creation of the world are clearly seen, being understood by the things that are made, even his eternal power and Godhead; so that they are without excuse. Because that, when they knew God, they glorified him not as God, neither were thankful; but became vain in their imaginations, and their foolish heart was darkened. Professing themselves to be wise, they became fools. (Romans 1:18–22)

> While we look not at the things which are seen, but at the things which are not seen: for the things which are seen are temporal; but the things which are not seen are eternal. (2 Corinthians 4:18)

> Looking unto Jesus the author and finisher of our faith; who for the joy that was set before him endured the cross, despising the shame, and is set down at the right hand of the throne of God. (Hebrews 12:2)

May we be overwhelmed at what we *see* and *understand* through real science and the truth that is revealed to us by God's Holy Spirit and through His Word. May we never again claim to be wise until we are first willing to become *foolish* in the eyes of the world.

Let us pray for our fellow "fish" living with us in our fishpond of life, who do not see what we see. Let us pray that they may gain *spiritual eyes* that they, too, might behold the glory of God.

· II ·

ATHEISM AND AGNOSTICISM: A PONDERING

We are all atheists about most of the gods that humanity has ever believed in. Some of us just go one god further.
—**Richard Dawkins**

As we think about those in the "fishpond" with us who, in particular, refuse to consider even the remotest possibility of the supernatural realm, let us take a moment and define some terms: namely, *atheism* and *agnosticism*.

You may be surprised to discover that the definition of atheism is not always an easy thing to pin down. One would think it should be rather straightforward. However, even within the atheist community, there are schisms and denominations of beliefs.

The broadest perception of *atheism* among atheists is, stated most correctly, *a lack of belief in any gods.* No specific claims or denials are made within this description. The *atheist* is simply one who does not happen to be a theist.

He makes no declaration as to *why* he does not believe. Nor does he state *how* he arrived at this monumental and perhaps eternal decision.

As you will discover in a moment, this is a truly insincere atheistic position. Yet a number of modern-day atheists choose to define themselves this way because in so doing, they assume they have built an impenetrable shield of protection around their position. After all, they say, "We are not declaring *why* we do not believe, only that we do not believe." They continue the ruse by saying, "Who are *you* to question what I believe or why I believe it?"

This general and broadest understanding of atheism is called *weak* or *implicit atheism.* Almost every modern dictionary begins its definition of atheism from this *weak* position.

However, a stronger genre of atheistic belief and declaration does exist. This variety of atheism is called *strong* or *explicit atheism.* In this definition, the atheist actually *denies* the existence of any gods, thus making a strong claim that *no god exists.* This position, obviously, requires a defense at some point in the atheist's argument.

Since, from a philosophical standpoint, this *strong* claim is refuted with relative ease, as will be demonstrated later, even the *strong atheist*, on occasion, will revert to the *weak atheist* argument in debating his position.

To further complicate the matter, a number of atheists make the *strong atheist* claim concerning certain *specific* gods but not others. Thus, a person may "lack belief" in one god but specifically deny the existence of another particular god altogether.

Before we proceed with this topic, let us examine a selection of trustworthy dictionary definitions, and then we will develop a *working definition* for the purpose of this book. Since we will encounter several variations of atheism within the atheistic community itself, I will attempt to produce a definition that best encompasses the general idea of what atheism actually represents.

Let us look at three reliable dictionary definitions. All three set forth comparable definitions, and all three represent both the *strong atheism* and the *weak atheism* definitions, although these specific terms are not used.

1. *Webster's Third New International Dictionary, Unabridged* (2002)
   Atheism: (from Greek atheos, "godless, not believing in the existence of gods)" 1a: disbelief in the existence of God or any other deity 1b: the doctrine that there is neither God nor any other deity 2: godlessness esp. in conduct: ungodliness, wickedness.

Notice how Webster's definition states the weak position in 1a and the strong position in 1b.

2. *Oxford English Dictionary*, 2nd ed. (Oxford University Press, March 30, 1989)
   Atheism: (from Greek atheos, "without God, denying God") Disbelief in, or denial of, the existence of a God. Also, disregard of duty to God, godlessness (practical atheism).

3. *The American Heritage Dictionary*, 3rd ed. (Dell Publishers, June 12, 1994)
   A·the·ism *n.* 1.a. Disbelief in or denial of the existence of God or gods. b. The doctrine that there is no God or gods.

2. Godlessness; immorality. [French athéisme, from athée, atheist, from Greek atheos, godless: a-, without]

WHO IS THIS UNBELIEVER?

Regardless of the specific definition we give to atheism, some atheists will always disagree with the definition. Nevertheless, I will venture a declaration. To be an atheist is, *at least*, to be one who declares he has no belief in God. In a logical sense, and by the majority of definitions, this lack of belief must be based upon a cognitive assertion. The most logical cognitive proposals for lack of belief in God are:

1. "I do not *want* to believe in a god." Atheism, thus stated, becomes a religion of convenience. It makes no logical sense to declare, "I just don't want to believe in God," without a qualification of the declaration. Certainly, everyone believes in *something* concerning God's existence, and there is *always* a reason or motivation for that belief. A human being does not make a decision devoid of rationale. It is simply not done—short of insanity, but that is another matter.

2. "I have made up my mind that there is no god." This is the *strong* atheist position, which insists there is no evidence for a god nor a logical argument for a god's existence; therefore, there *cannot be* a god. The reasonable conclusion one could draw for why someone would arrive at this definitive declaration is that the atheist has studied the issue thoroughly and has concluded without a doubt that there is no god in existence—anywhere. The Bible is clear in addressing this reckless approach to theology: "The fool hath said in his heart, There is no God." (Psalm 14:1)

Our working definition of atheism will encompass both the weak and strong positions. For our purposes, an atheist is one who proclaims: "I do not believe in a god or gods because I have either cognitively concluded there is none, or I have simply decided I do not *want* there to be a god or gods."

Again, some atheists will object even to this all-inclusive definition. They wish instead to construct a definition of who they are and what they believe that, in effect, *has no definition*, no *reason*, so it cannot be attacked with sound logic. This is nothing more than convenient and purposed *evasion*.

If I claim I am a Christian because I have *chosen* to be a Christian, then you might ask, "*Why* did you choose, and *how* did you choose to be Christian? You *must* have a reason why you made that choice." My reason could be as simple as, "Because it was the way I was raised." That is an acceptable and honest reason.

However, if I assert that I have no reason whatsoever for making such a choice, then my statement is relegated to absurdity—or perhaps insanity. Moreover, the estimation of my intelligence would take a severe plunge. Hence, the atheist who says he does not believe in God only because he *chooses* not to is engaging in nothing more than atheistic double talk.

While engaging in abundant debates with the atheist community, I frequently encounter the following adage: *Atheism is the most natural state of man.* The atheist's claim here is that religion has to be either learned or imposed upon a person, because in our most *natural* state, we are nonreligious or atheistic.

From this logic, then, many atheists conclude that everyone actually begins as an atheist, and becomes religious only by outside influence. The implication is that if someone believes in a god, or gods, it is only because he has been forced or taught to do so against every fiber of common sense embedded within his nature.

I estimate that factual human experience and clear biblical declaration refute this idea. However, even if the assertion were true, the atheist still has a monumental dilemma.

According to the latest statistics, the vast majority of the world's population is religious, to one degree or another, and believes in God, a god, or several gods. This means that more atheists have become religious, and have even become Christian, by far, than Christians have become atheists. In other words, the atheist is losing his evangelistic battle of endeavor, and religion is winning.

As it turns out, then, the atheist may *wish*, and even insist, that our most natural inclination is to be atheistic, but the statistics bear out that our most natural inclination is to be religious. Therefore, the natural inclination of man, in reality, is to *reject* atheism.

Thus, Richard Dawkins' statement at the beginning of this chapter ("We are all atheists about most of the gods that humanity has ever believed in. Some of us just go one god further") is true, but is not one about which he should brag.

Dr. Dawkins proclaims that each individual ultimately makes a decision about whether or not he will believe in a god or gods. In so doing, he will reject all other gods and settle in on the god(s) of his choice. However, boasts Dawkins, the atheist goes one step further in this rejection process until he has finally rejected *all* gods.

Dr. Dawkins maintains that this position is the most natural and enlightened one. Nevertheless, as we have just demonstrated, though his quote is cute, touched with a humorous note of sarcasm, it is also mistaken and flawed from the standpoint of logic.

Naturally, our desire as Christians is to make sure that as many people as possible, who are merely steeped in religion, come to understand the truth about who God is and how He has represented His offer of salvation through Jesus Christ.

HOW MANY OF THEM ARE THERE—REALLY?

A survey set forth in the *Encyclopedia Britannica* indicates that the nonreligious of the world's population numbered about 14.7 percent in 1995, while atheists numbered around 3.8 percent.[1] A 2004 survey by the CIA in the *World Factbook*[2] estimates that about 12.5 percent of the world's population is nonreligious. Of those, only about 2.4 percent define themselves as atheists.

The *nonreligious* are those who are not defined as atheists but, rather, as those who are open to the likelihood of the existence of a god but do not practice a particular religious expression of that belief. In other words, they have chosen to make no expression of belief in God.

A 2004 survey by the Pew Research Center showed that in the United States, only about 12 percent of people under the age of thirty and 6 percent of people over the age of thirty could be characterized as nonreligious.[3]

A 2005 poll by AP/Ipsos surveyed ten countries,[4] and the results are enlightening. Among the developed nations, the United States was most certain of the existence of God: only 2 percent of respondents were atheists, and 4 percent were agnostic. France had the majority of cynics: 19 percent atheist, and 16 percent agnostic. South Korea, at 41 percent, had the greatest proportion of respondents who lacked a religious conviction of any type, while Italy had the lowest rate of religious certainty, at 5 percent.

The best statistics we possess seem to indicate that a full 97 to 98 percent of the world's population believes in some sort of "god"(s), as opposed to only about 2 to 3 percent who claim to be atheists. In addition, the latest statistical studies and polls also indicate that while there are more atheists than ever before, by total number (merely because the world's population has grown significantly), atheism's overall *percentages* of total world population are in a noticeable decline.

Regardless of what year you may be reading this book, even if it is decades beyond the research dates just listed, the trends have been the same for numerous years. I doubt they will be much different in the future.

THE SAGA OF THE FOUR-HEADED FROG

Now let us consider the philosophical and theological implications of the belief system whose adherents announce, "I do not believe in a god or gods because I have concluded that there is none.

What if I made the statement, "I do not believe there are any four-headed frogs on the island of Oahu. I hold this belief because I have definitively concluded that my belief is correct." What would be your initial reaction?

I assume you would have a few questions for me. This statement of unbelief in such a frog would be reasonable in that, to date, no one has ever offered for observation a four-headed frog coming from the island of Oahu. To my best knowledge, a four-headed frog has not been observed *anywhere* in the world or at any time in human history.

However, what if abundant stories and testimonies proclaimed that a four-headed frog from Oahu, in actuality, had been seen? What if books had been written (absent photos) about a four-headed frog that lives somewhere in the forests and mountains of Oahu? Still, the belief that no such frog exists could be set forth with reason since no one has one in possession for immediate observation. In fact, even the statement, "I do not believe in a four-headed frog because it is silly beyond comprehension to believe in such a creature," is reasonable. However, one would have to admit that the wisest and most intelligent thing to say in this case, and in light of the anecdotal evidence for the frog's possible existence, would be something like this: "I think it is silly to believe in a four-headed frog. I do not believe in the existence of such a creature; however, I do leave open the possibility that such a creature could exist."

The majority of atheists do not come close to making a statement that affirms even the *possibility* of God's existence. I call those who do *honest atheists*. Most, however, are not honest atheists. After all, the crux of the entire atheistic position is that God does not exist. This is the conclusion they have made. This is why I maintain that the atheistic position is, at the very least, dishonest. I will address the irrefutable evidence for the existence of God in the next chapter.

What if my statement about the frog was ratcheted up a notch, to, "I do not believe in a four-headed frog existing on the island of Oahu. I can categorically state that no such frog exists. There is no such creature. I know this as fact." Of course, you now recognize this to be more akin to the *strong atheist* position. This position states there is no God—period. Since, to the atheist, there is no God and the concept of His existence is silly from its premise, strong atheists would say their belief is justified.

This type of *strong atheistic* statement is the same as me saying, "There are no four-headed frogs on Oahu, and I know this for a fact." Now, a different level of thought must be employed.

To make a categorical statement such as this assumes several weighty implications. To emphatically declare that *there are no four-headed frogs* on the island of Oahu implies that I have conducted a survey of every single square inch of the island and have demonstrated that no such frog exists. Even in a small area such as the island of Oahu, this would be an almost impossible task.

How much more impossible would it be to make a personal search for the Creator God through all the vast and unending heavens and all the dimensions of reality now being exposed through quantum understanding? What about the dimensions that exist but are yet to be discovered? What of the dimensions that we may never discover? What about those dimensions we might be incapable of comprehending? Is there a possibility, even the slightest, that God *does* exist in some area of exploration where the atheist has not and perhaps cannot yet travel? Several statistical formulations say there is at least a logical probability of God's existence. Even my *fishpond* illustration demonstrates this.

The saga of the four-headed frog leaves the atheist in a quandary. Either position he takes, weak or strong, leaves him looking at least dishonest and perhaps blatantly foolish. If he takes the weak position without being honest enough to admit he could be mistaken, he appears disingenuous. If he takes the strong stance and stands upon it like a rock, he appears obviously foolish.

PONDERING THE MIND OF AN ATHEIST

What happens if the atheist, at the end of the day, is overwhelmed by the majesty, complexity, and mathematical impossibilities of the random accumulation of more than two million intricate and varied species of life that are undeniably displayed before his eyes? What does he think as he contemplates the intricacy of the ecology that surrounds and sustains that life—when he looks at the quantum level and marvels at the irreducible complexity of it all? What happens when he reflects on the absolute necessity of the unbelievable, improbable, and unpredictable quanta activities, law, and forces that are required to sustain his own insignificant life?

What does he imagine when he looks into the farthest reaches of the universe in an attempt to find life, any life, even an iota of life, somewhere, anywhere else, in the vastness of the endless array of galaxies—and he finds *none*?

When the atheist is overwhelmed by the incomprehensible

vastness of what he sees, the sheer power of all that lies before him, the majesty that spreads out like a canopy over him, and the unfathomable insignificance of the next breath he takes or the next beat of his lowly heart, what does he think?

What happens when he considers the monumental improbabilities of the intricate grandeur of life he observes, day by day, contained on merely one known planet in the universe—this little floating rock upon which he lives? When he is besieged with wonderment and then, ultimately, with gratitude—to *whom* does the atheist give thanks?

What happens if the atheist becomes an activist and protests against everything Christian, everything biblical? If the God against whom he so vigorously protests does not exist in his little fishpond of possibilities, and if he is *certain* of it, then why, may I ask, does he protest with such ferociousness against Him? Is such illogical protestation not just one definition of insanity?

I have concluded that it, indeed, is a fortuitous situation that God *does* exist—lest the atheist would have little purpose in life.

Now, let us discuss the position of the agnostic.

THE ULTIMATE "FENCE SITTER"

The English term *agnostic* is a derivative of the Greek word *agnostos*, meaning "to not know." The prefix *a* means "not" or "without." The word *gnosis* means "knowledge." Therefore, an agnostic is one who acknowledges, "I don't know" or "I am without knowledge." The term is applied, in specific, to those who claim they do not know with certainty whether God exists. An agnostic, then, says he believes the existence of God is unknown and beyond human ability to discover.

By definition, then, an agnostic is not devoted to believing or disbelieving in the reality of God. While agnosticism strives to *sit on the fence*, countless agnostics are, in reality, *practical atheists*. That is to say, they pursue the *atheistic* lifestyle. In so doing, they tend to subscribe to moral relativism and live their lives without concern for ultimate accountability. In other words, the agnostic is rather happy to sit on the fence and ask that he be *left alone* in his satisfied state of *unknowing*.

This state of unknowing is where I think the believer may make a few inroads toward assisting the agnostic in his unbelief or uncertainty. For the agnostic is sometimes honest enough to admit that God may exist. If he is honest, all he is saying is that right now he is not certain if there is a God.

The agnostic will often say he would believe in God if one could, without a doubt, *prove* His existence. He says this with a certain degree of smugness, believing the Christian cannot possibly prove the existence of God. Nothing could be farther from the truth.

As you will see in the following chapter, contrary to the words of Pastor Jim in chapter 1, one *can* prove the existence of God. In fact, the logical, historical, scientific, and verified evidence for God's existence is irrefutable. The proof is before our eyes every single day. The evidence has existed for thousands of years. Would you like to know what the proof is?

· 12 ·

PROVING THE EXISTENCE
OF GOD: THE SET-UP

"If you can prove the existence of God, then I will believe in Him. But I know you can't prove His existence, because it is impossible to do so."

W ith this declaration, the biblical antagonist thinks he is safe. You will soon discover, however, that no one who makes this declaration will ever again be *safe*. The agnostics' request for proof is granted with ease, and they will not be able to logically dispute it. Furthermore, they will be forever accountable to God for what they now understand.

WARNING: If you are a professing *unbeliever*—you may

wish to read no further.

This claim is made not to be trite or presumptuous but rather to declare what God Himself has said. He has *proven* His existence, and He has done it in plain fashion and without dispute. He further declares that He has done so in such a profound manner that not only will you be certain that He exists and that He is God, but you will also be forced to confess that He *alone* is God.

God has made this claim about Himself. I am merely repeating and elucidating what He has asserted and what He, in fact, has done. This is indeed a bold and profound assertion. However, He has accomplished an undeniable and supernatural feat. We are now without excuse.

THE BASIS FOR THE PROOF

Before we reveal concrete proof for God's existence, we must first discuss the platform from which we will launch our revelation. At the core of biblical Christianity is the Bible itself. The Bible is like no other book in the world. To this day, it is the best-selling book on the planet and the best-selling book in the history of humanity. No other book comes close.

The Old Testament contains dozens of distinctive prophecies about a *coming One*. The people of God had been in possession of the entirety of the Old Testament documents, as we now have them, for at least several hundred years before the Christ event.

The ancient prophecies speak of the Christ's birthplace, the exact time of His coming, His work, His miracles, His teachings, and His death. They describe the type of death He would suffer, the magnitude of His suffering, and His resurrection. All of these prophecies were recorded hundreds of years, and several of them thousands of years, before they were actually fulfilled.

Out of the seven billion people alive today and the billions who have lived before, just one man has ever fulfilled every one of the biblical prophecies concerning the coming of the Christ. They were fulfilled, exclusively, in the person of Jesus of Nazareth—Jesus the Christ. The statistical improbability of this historically actualized phenomenon is staggering.

No other book known to man has dared to speak such presumptuous prophecies. No other book contains such prophecies that have now been fulfilled and are continually open to the scrutiny of the world. This fact does not include the scores and scores of other prophecies found in the Bible concerning nations, kings, people groups, coming events, the second coming of the Christ, and Christ's ultimate reign upon the earth.

No other book is scrutinized in the same way, yet stands the test of time and detraction. Not a single archaeological discovery in the history of the science of uncovering ancient artifacts has ever proven a single stated fact of the Bible to be incorrect. The Bible has presided, in time, over the death of every one of its detractors. They are gone, yet the Bible still lives.

The sixty-six books of the Bible were written over a period of about fifteen hundred years, by more than forty different authors. The authors wrote at different times, to different audiences, about a diverse variety of spiritual and eternal matters. Yet, their communication is a singular and flowing, congruent message without contradiction or error. The books of the Bible, in their original form, were written in four different languages: Hebrew, Chaldean, Greek, and Aramaic. The manuscripts of the Bible were copied by hand for thousands of years, reproduced several thousands of times, and then distributed in a far-reaching fashion throughout the world. Yet, we still have them preserved with striking accuracy, as recent discoveries like the Qumran Texts and the Dead Sea Scrolls have demonstrated. The Bible proposes definitive answers and unyielding conclusions regarding hundreds of controversial topics, including profound statements regarding life, death, heaven, hell, eternity, sin, creation, morality, eternal accountability, and prophecy. Even so, its message is fluid and harmonious from Genesis to Revelation. The possibility that the Bible would exist as a continued work, considering all of the aforementioned factors, is a statistical conundrum. Yet it does exist, and it continues to outsell all other books.

The New Testament documents are about two thousand years old. The earliest of the documents was written around the 40s AD, and the latest in the 90s AD. All of them were written within about a fifty-year period, and within the lifetimes of the first generation of the early Christians, or very shortly thereafter. Many of these first-generation Christians who saw and examined these documents were actual eyewitnesses of the events they purport to record.

> For I delivered unto you first of all that which I also received, how that Christ died for our sins according to the scriptures; and that he was buried, and that he rose again the third day according to the scriptures: and that he was seen of Cephas, then of the twelve: After that, he was seen of above five hundred brethren at once; of whom the greater part remain unto this present, but some are fallen asleep. (1 Corinthians 15:3–6)

Furthermore, we are in possession of more than twenty-four thousand partial or complete manuscript copies of the New Testament documents, as well as more than eighty-six thousand quotes from the biblical documents that were used by the early church fathers and preserved in their writings. The copious quotes confirm the veracity and accuracy of the documents.

We must note that we have few reliable documents coming out of the same period that dispute the accuracy or truthfulness of the New Testament's recorded attestations. With the monumental claims made within these widely circulated and scrutinized biblical documents, there is at least a possibility that *someone* would have disputed them if their claims were false. In fact, considering the audacity of the New Testament claims, a reasonable person would assume there would have been vast amounts of materials arising out of the first century that disputed the claims.

While I should think that there must have been *someone* living in that day who questioned the *methods* of Jesus' miracles, for example, apparently there was not an uproar questioning the fact that He *performed* the miracles.

Not even His crucifixion could be disputed with any degree of reasonableness. This was a well-known public event. Vast crowds cried out for His execution. Numerous people from these same crowds *witnessed* His execution. I am unaware of any historical records that document anyone surviving a Roman crucifixion. The still-living victim's legs were often broken to ensure a swift suffocation and certain death. Spears were thrust into the sides of the victims, up and into the heart and lungs.

A Roman governor ordered Jesus' execution. Roman officials were assigned to carry out the task. A company of Roman soldiers was given the task of guarding the tomb. None of this was done in secret or in a sloppy or halfhearted fashion.

While some may question the veracity of the resurrection of Jesus, there is no dispute that His body has never been discovered. It disappeared only three short days after the crucifixion, right from under the noses of a company of Roman soldiers. The soldiers were guarding the body under penalty of severe punishment, yet it vanished—in spite of the careful and watchful scrutiny of the Jewish leaders who ordered the execution. In particular, they had *everything* to lose by the body going missing. They feared His missing body infinitely more than they feared His life and work. One would assume that the mighty, invincible, Roman military could guard a buried, encased, sealed, and dead Jewish rabbi's body for three short days without losing it. Would a detractor of the resurrection really suggest that a ragtag band of Galilean anglers and religious disciples could steal the body from under the nose of the Roman government, with its overwhelming military might?

> Now the next day, that followed the day of the preparation, the chief priests and Pharisees came together unto Pilate, saying, Sir, we remember that that deceiver said, while he was yet alive, After three days I will rise again. Command therefore that the sepulchre be made sure until the third day, lest his disciples come by night, and steal him away, and say unto the people, He is risen from the dead: so the last error shall be worse than the first.
>
> Pilate said unto them, Ye have a watch: go your way, make it as sure as ye can. So they went, and made the sepulchre sure, sealing the stone, and setting a watch. (Matthew 27:62–66)

It is not probable that the body was stolen or that a trick was performed under such circumstances. To make a claim of this enormity is to make a claim of the highest speculation with the least evidence.

Even historical writings years after the Jesus event recorded the factual existence of the man named Jesus of Nazareth. These attestations record His miracles, His teachings, His crucifixion, and His resurrection, or at least the claim of it.

Once more, no other book records such stupendous events in the name of God. The Hindu Veda does not come close. The writings of Confucius do not compare to the Bible. The cryptic writings of Nostradamus do not hold a candle to the Bible and its claims. Even the Quran, the holy book of the Muslim world, contains nothing of the majesty, the magnitude, and the historical veracity and authenticity of the Holy Bible. There is no other book anywhere in the world that rains such monumental claims upon an individual's life.

The Bible asserts that we are sinners, lost and bound for an eternal hell. It claims that our singular hope of salvation is through a born-again relationship with Jesus Christ. It declares the existence of a heaven and a hell, and that a divine judgment is soon to come upon the world. The Bible further maintains that man is accountable for his own life and his own actions before a holy, omnipotent, Creator God. Undoubtedly, it is claims such as these that cause the Bible to be despised and feared by so many.

The preceding facts about the Bible have not been presented here as the *proof* for God's existence. God did not say that any of the facts that were earlier stated were the ultimate proof for His existence. As marvelous as the *coming One* prophecies and their fulfillment in Jesus Christ are, they are not God's stated proof that He exists.

Moreover, Jesus' death on the cross and even His resurrection are not God's stated proof for His existence. They *are* proofs of His love, His promised and fulfilled work of redemption, and even of the *second* coming of Jesus, which will be accompanied by His divine judgment—but they still do not prove that God *is*.

Again, the reason I spent a good deal of time examining the reliability of the Bible is because the Bible will be the launching pad for God's proof of His existence. Once we have launched, you will discover that irrefutable proof also exists outside of biblical sources. However, only the Bible has first recorded the proof, long before it happened.

A MATTER OF FAITH

> Now faith is the substance of things hoped for, the evidence of things not seen. For by it the elders [saints in the past] obtained a good report [were commended]. (Hebrews 11:1–2)

I find it astonishing when a Christian—and in particular a preacher, teacher, or Bible professor, says we cannot *prove* the existence of God. First, God *Himself* says that He has proven His existence—in an undeniable way. If *He* has done it, should not we proclaim it too? We will examine God's evidence in more detail in the following pages. However, for now, ask yourself, does it not make sense, if God is omniscient, omnipresent, and omnipotent, that He *could* prove His existence to mere mortals? If He is the loving God He claims to be, would He not *want* to prove Himself to the creation He claims He loves?

The answer to each of these questions is a resounding *yes*. This is why it is surprising when I hear fellow Christians and Bible expositors claim that God's existence cannot be proven.

When someone asks, "Can you prove the existence of God?" I often hear the following passage quoted: "But without faith it is impossible to please him: for he that cometh to God must believe that he is, and that he is a rewarder of them that diligently seek him." (Hebrews 11:6)

Typically, this verse is interpreted to mean: *One cannot prove the existence of God. Belief in God has to be taken on simple faith. We have to believe that He exists by faith and faith alone.* The pastor in chapter 1 gave our poor, beat-up, college-attending Christian this answer. It did nothing to bolster his already wavering and challenged faith.

The problem is, this is not what that verse says at all. The preceding interpretation is not the contextual understanding of the intended message. Carefully look at the words of this verse again.

There is nothing expressed in this passage of scripture about proving God's existence. The first part says that we cannot please God without *faith*. In the simplest biblical definition, faith is *taking God at His Word.* Unless you believe God's Word and take it as truth, you cannot please God. I understand that. I am certain that you do as well.

The second part of the verse declares that anyone who comes to Him must believe He exists. Of course, one cannot come to someone whose very existence he doubts in the first place. How, then, do we believe that God exists? The passage does not address that matter. As you will soon see, the Bible *does* address the matter of how we can be certain He exists, but this particular passage simply proclaims that one must first *believe* that God exists, and then one can come to Him. It presupposes that you believe He exists, and you understand *why* you believe. When you do come to Him, you must live for Him by obeying His Word. This is faith. If you cannot come to Him and live for Him in faith and obedience, you cannot please Him.

This understanding of faith is the context of the whole of chapter 11 of Hebrews. Nothing is emphasized in this chapter about *proving* God's existence. It takes for granted that God's *existence* is not a question. So *the* real question and message of the passage is, *"Will you live for God in faith, no matter what comes your way, no matter what He asks you to do?"* If you cannot live this way, you cannot possibly please God. *This is what the ancients were commended for*, not for believing in or proving the existence of God, but for following Him *in faith*—even if their obedience cost them their popularity with the masses, or their lives. God's existence was never in question.

So, what is God's *own* proof of His existence? What was it that He chose to hold out to His creation as evidence of His reality? The answer might surprise you. It is as plain as the nose on your face. It is before us every day, yet the majority of the world misses it. In the next chapter, you will see it clearly.

· 13 ·

PROVING THE EXISTENCE OF GOD: THE DELIVERY

Unto thee it was shewed, that thou mightest know that the LORD he is God; there is none else beside him.
—Deuteronomy 4:35

God's own evidence proves His existence and, at the same time, proves He is the *only* God. He also authoritatively proves that the Bible is the true and exclusive Word of the living God. His proof of Himself begins with the following passage:

For ask now of the days that are past, which were before thee, since the day that God created man upon the earth, and ask from the one side of heaven unto the other, whether there hath been any such thing as this great thing is, or hath been heard like it? Did ever people hear the voice of God speaking out of the midst of the fire, as thou hast heard, and live? Or hath God assayed to go and take him a nation from the midst of another nation, by temptations, by signs, and by wonders, and by war, and by a mighty hand, and by a stretched out arm, and by great terrors, according to all that the LORD your God did for you in Egypt before your eyes? Unto thee it was shewed, that thou mightest know that the LORD he is God; there is none else beside him. Out of heaven he made thee to hear his voice, that he might instruct thee: and upon earth he shewed thee his great fire; and thou heardest his words out of the midst of the fire. And because he loved thy fathers, therefore he chose their seed after them, and brought thee out in his sight with his mighty power out of Egypt; to drive out nations from before thee greater and mightier than thou art, to bring thee in, to give thee their land for an inheritance, as it is this day. Know therefore this day, and consider it in thine heart, that the LORD he is God in heaven above, and upon the earth beneath: there is none else. (Deuteronomy 4:32–39)

Did you see it? It is there before our eyes. The Bible declares, "Unto thee it was shewed, that thou mightest know that the LORD he is God; there is none else beside him."

What *things* have we been shown? What is the context here? Of what is God speaking? The beginning of the answer is revealed in verse 34: "Or hath God assayed to go and take him a nation from the midst of another nation?"

There it is; God's *proof* of His existence! This declaration is divine evidence that He is the one and only God. This is also His proof that the Bible, which declares this truth, was the only book that had ever proclaimed such a certainty. His proof is the nation of *Israel.*

Let me explain. Though this revelation may not appear so insightful right now, it will in a moment. The proof is undeniable. It will serve you well to thoroughly understand it.

The context of this passage is that God was just getting ready to take His children, the Israelites, into the Promised Land. This would happen under the leadership of Joshua. However, Moses was now giving the final instructions to God's people after forty years of wandering and preparation in the wilderness.

Not long after He gave these instructions, Moses died. Joshua then took the Israelites across the Jordan River and into Canaan. The immediate context of *"You were shown these things"* is that of the miraculous deliverance of and provision for the children of Israel whom God had brought out of Egypt.

What God *had* done, what He *was then* doing, and what He *would do* with the nation of Israel down through the ages would be the proof that He is God, and there is no other. Now prepare for a real shocker.

Before they entered the Promised Land, settled the land according to their tribes, became a nation of any kind, or ever had their first king, Moses prophesied about Israel's *future.* The prophecy is startling, for it not only foretells of Israel's future disobedience but also of its future scattering among the nations as God's punishment for their disobedience. Of all things contained within this prediction is also a prophecy that Israel would one day *return* to the land from where they had been scattered. Once they returned and settled it, the nation of Israel would be revived!

This startling declaration and its fulfillment were to be part of God's *proof* to the world that He is God, the LORD God of the Bible, and no other *gods* exist. When the prophecy happened, it would further prove that His word is *trustworthy* and final.

All of this was given in prophecy before the Israelites ever set one foot on the Promised Land. That fact is enormous. Moreover, that the prophecy was given three thousand years before it was fulfilled is an undeniable fact of history. It is recorded in the book of Deuteronomy, chapter 30:

> And it shall come to pass, when all these things are come upon thee, the blessing and the curse, which I have set before thee, and thou shalt call them to mind among all the nations, whither the LORD thy God hath driven thee, and shalt return unto the LORD thy God, and shalt obey his voice according to all that I command thee this day, thou and thy children, with all thine heart, and with all thy soul; that then the LORD thy God will turn thy captivity, and have compassion upon thee, and will return and gather thee from all the nations, whither the LORD thy God hath scattered thee. If any of thine be driven out unto the outmost parts of heaven, from thence will the LORD thy God gather thee, and from thence will he fetch thee: and the LORD thy God will bring thee into the land which thy fathers possessed, and thou shalt possess it; and he will do thee good, and multiply thee above thy fathers. (30:1–5)

Of course, we now live on the other side of the prophecy of Deuteronomy 30. Israel did rebel. The nation was driven from the land, and, as the passage predicted, Israel has now returned to the land from which it was driven. This fact makes the first declaration of Deuteronomy 4 all the more profound. I am afraid I cannot do proper justice to what you read in Deuteronomy 4. In an attempt to do so let me reemphasize several of the passage's important truths.

God, through His servant Moses, foretold what He would do with the nation of Israel. These experiences were to be a sign to the world—believing and unbelieving ("among all the nations")—that what God says is *true*—including the fact that "the LORD he is God; there is none else beside him" (4:35).

"Has any other god ever done such a thing," God asks. The answer is obvious, without dispute. Not a single other *god* ever did such a thing—not Buddha, not Allah, not Baal—not any *god.* Only the God of the Bible declared that He would take a specific people and turn them into a mighty nation. He even promised that out of this nation He would bring His blessings to the world:

> And I will bless them that bless thee, and curse him that curseth thee: and in thee shall all families of the earth be blessed. (Genesis 12:3)

What has come out of Israel as a blessing? To name a few: the Word of God, the prophecies of God, the prophecies of the Messiah, the coming of the Messiah, Calvary's cross, the empty tomb, the gospel message, the birth of the Church, and the giving of the Holy Spirit—all are essential in man's eternal salvation, and all came out of Israel. God kept His promise. No other God has ever claimed such a thing.

Now, let us further contemplate the *history* of the nation of Israel. Remember, the *way* God dealt with Israel would be His sign to the world and proof that He exists and that there is no god beside Him (Deuteronomy 4:32–35).

ISRAEL'S PROPHETIC JOURNEY

Following are those things of which we are certain concerning Israel's journey. Remember, the words of Deuteronomy were given long before these events happened.

Israel did indeed settle the land of Canaan. They inhabited that land for more than three hundred years as it was settled according to the twelve tribes.

After the period of the *judges,* Israel went to a system of *kings.* Saul was the first king, David the second, and Solomon the third.

King Solomon built the temple of the Lord in Jerusalem. David had earlier conquered Jerusalem, made it the capital of Israel, reestablished the tabernacle sacrifices, and placed the Ark of the Covenant there. David and Solomon established Israel as one of the mightiest superpowers of the world in their day. They were the force with which to be reckoned. Their power, military might, wealth, economy, and influence upon the area were unquestioned. The borders of the nation of Israel were expanded in a tremendous way under the reigns of these two kings.

After the reign of King Solomon, Israel underwent a civil war. The war, in the end, resulted in the establishment of two Hebrew kingdoms. The *Northern Kingdom* was known as Israel, with its capital located at Samaria. The *Southern Kingdom* was known as Judah, with its capital located at Jerusalem.

The undoing of the Northern Kingdom was the eventual rise of the Assyrian superpower. God raised up prophets to warn the kings of both the north and the south that if they did not repent of their evil ways, the ominous prophesies of Israel's demise would soon fall upon them. Israel did not repent. Assyria swept down and destroyed the Northern Kingdom's reign. They carried into captivity the ten tribes of the Northern Kingdom.

The Babylonian Empire eventually overwhelmed and con-quered the Assyrian Empire. Several decades later, under King Nebuchadnezzar, the Babylonian Kingdom conquered the Southern Kingdom of Judah. Again, this happened only after much preaching and warning from the prophets. Judah did not heed the Word of the Lord either. The Babylonians then carried the remaining two tribes of Israel into captivity.

The temple of the Lord was looted and destroyed; the city walls and gates of Jerusalem were also destroyed. By this time in history, neither the Northern nor the Southern Kingdom remained. Israel as a nation was now gone; it was scattered to the heathen nations. All of this happened just as Moses prophesied it would. It is astounding to note again that Moses gave the prophecy before the Israelites entered the Promised Land. Babylon conquered Judah in 586 BC. God's *proof* was happening before the eyes of the world.

Many years later, the Persian Empire conquered the Babylonian Empire and ruled that part of the world. A number of Jews living within the new Persian Empire were allowed to return to their homeland and rebuild part of the city of Jerusalem and the Temple. The Jews were not allowed to rule themselves, however. They were not yet an independent nation. Countless Jews who were in captivity did not return to the land.

Centuries later, the Greeks ruled the entire known world after defeating the Persians under the conquering efforts of Alexander the Great. You may recall from a previous chapter that Alexander the Great was taught by Aristotle that *spontaneous generation* was the *scientific* stuff of life. I remind you of this so you will have a sense of the historical context of when that pseudoscientific belief became prevalent. (In spite of its unscientific nature, it is still the prevailing thought in evolutionary *origins theory* today.)

Now back to Israel's history and God's proof of His existence. The next empire to rule the world was the Roman Empire. Under the Roman general Pompey in 63 BC, the area of ancient Israel was conquered for Rome. The Caesars now ruled the hodgepodge of people who lived there. Numerous Jews were living in the land alongside people of various other cultures and races. These diverse people groups accumulated in the area down through the ages and under the different ruling empires.

Keep in mind that by this time in history, called the Roman period, Israel had not been a nation since the Babylonians conquered them almost five hundred years earlier.

During this Roman period of world history, God stepped

into humanity in the person of Jesus Christ, thus fulfilling the dozens of prophecies of the coming of the Messiah. The New Testament documents were written during this period, all of them within the years of the first century.

Almost forty years after the Christ event in AD 70, the Romans destroyed the remnants of the rebuilt temple in Jerusalem and further dispersed the remaining Jews from the area of Judea. They did this in response to a popular religious and political uprising of the Jewish people. Rome, having had enough of such uprisings, drove the Jews from the land.

This dispersion would take several decades. However, over time and with great resolve, a succession of Roman Caesars would follow through on the endeavor of ridding the land of all Jews.

In AD 135, to further dissuade the Jews from returning to or living in the land, the Roman emperor Hadrian placed the name *Palestine* on the area that was formerly the nation of Israel. *Palestine* is a Latin word, meaning the *land of the Philistines.* The Philistines had been one of Israel's most hated enemies since the earliest of times. Hadrian surmised that naming it thus would so repulse the Jews that they would not want to live there again.

By the way, the popular and political practice of today's media in calling the Arabs who live or used to live in the land *Palestinians* is without a doubt a woeful and incorrect usage of the word. The Arab people who live there are not even remotely related to the ancient Philistines. In a technical sense, *anyone* who has lived in that land for any length of time could be called a *Palestinian* under the old Roman designation—including the Jews. Before Israel became a nation, the media routinely referred to Jews who lived in that area of the world as the *Palestinian Jews*.

Not until after World War II would the United Nations, in conjunction with England, France, and the United States, declare a certain portion of "Palestine" to be reserved for the Jewish people to live. The remaining portion was reserved for the Arab people. The Jews agreed to the designated areas; the Arabs did not.

THEN THE UNBELIEVABLE HAPPENED

On May 14, 1948, Israel declared itself an independent nation. The following day, a confederation of several Arab nations attacked the brand-new country. A little over a year and a half later, Israel emerged as the victor. The new nation was then firmly established. Israel returned to the land in the precise way that Moses and numerous prophets after him foretold. Knowing this ahead of time, God had claimed that when it happened, they would know that He was the one and *only* God:

> I will say to the north, Give up; and to the south, Keep not back: bring my sons from far, and my daughters from the ends of the earth . . . that ye may know and believe me, and understand that I am he: before me there was no God formed, neither shall there be after me. I, even I, am the LORD; and beside me there is no saviour. (Isaiah 43:6, 10–11)

The world saw it occur, and we are witnesses of the miracle even today. Never before in human history has such impossibility among the affairs of nations occurred. However, the impossible did occur with Israel, and the whole world saw it, so now they know without excuse that He alone is LORD.

Think of this: No other nation in the history of the world has ever been dispersed and scattered among other nations for almost twenty-five hundred years and then returned to their land. Not only did they return, but they also reestablished their borders, government, heritage, traditions, power, economy, and status in the world as a nation. Nothing like this has ever happened before, and nothing like this among the nations will ever happen again.

This is a unique event of human history—and it is recorded in our Bibles as well as in the secular history books and observed on our television sets every night. God's evidence has been set before our eyes in an undeniable way.

AGAINST ALL ODDS

In case I have not done justice to the magnitude of this truth, consider this illustration:

What if the United States of America was conquered and overrun by an emerging world superpower? What if the conquering nation's military carried away all 300-plus million Americans from our country and deposited almost every one of us in the remote backcountry of a faraway land and dispersed the rest of us across the various nations of the world?

What if for the next twenty-five hundred years, our descendants intermarried and lived among a multiplicity of nations and cultures? What would be the odds that two and a half millennia later our descendants would decide to return to the shores of America? What would be the odds that they would restore its borders, government, capitol, Constitution, language, institutions, culture, military might, and economic power, and that the glory of America could rise again after such a devastating blow from the conquering nation, especially given the ensuing passage of time?

This scenario is utterly unthinkable and would be humanly *impossible*. Why would people from several generations into the future know or care about the ancient America of their ancestors? How could they pull off such an unachievable feat? Without a doubt, this undertaking could not be accomplished.

No other nation in the history of humanity has *ever* accomplished such a thing—except Israel.

Consider also the prophetic words of Ezekiel, who lived and

prophesied in the land of Judah. He foretold of Judah's destruction at the hands of Babylon, declaring that it would surely occur
if the kings and the people of Judah failed to repent from their
wicked ways. They did not repent, and Ezekiel foresaw the ultimate annihilation of Israel and the subsequent thousands of years
of dispersion. God then showed Ezekiel a vision known to Bible
students as the vision of the *Valley of the Dry Bones.*

In this astounding vision, Ezekiel was shown in dramatic
fashion the rebuilding of Israel and its glory in the last days. In
Ezckiel's vision, the Lord declares, yet again, that when this
miraculous restoration happened, the world would know that He
was the Lord who had spoken it. Ponder the words of this vision:

> Again he said unto me, Prophesy upon these bones, and
> say unto them, O ye dry bones, hear the word of the LORD.
> Thus saith the Lord GOD unto these bones; Behold, I will
> cause breath to enter into you, and ye shall live. . . . Then he
> said unto me, Son of man, these bones are the whole house
> of Israel: behold, they say, Our bones are dried, and our
> hope is lost: we are cut off for our parts. Therefore prophesy
> and say unto them, Thus saith the Lord GOD; behold, O
> my people, I will open your graves, and cause you to come
> up out of your graves, and bring you into the land of Israel.
> And ye shall know that I am the LORD, when I have opened
> your graves, O my people, and brought you up out of your
> graves, and shall put my spirit in you, and ye shall live, and
> I shall place you in your own land: then shall ye know that I
> the LORD have spoken it, and performed it, saith the LORD.
> (Ezekiel 37:4–5, 11–14)

This is the certain evidence for which the unbelieving world
has been asking. It is also the evidence for which the Christian
community has been *wishing*. Yet, it has been present all along,
and the Lord Himself declared it would be so.

Now the evidence is before us. God affirmed thousands of years before it happened that He would do something with the nation of Israel that the entire world would see. He proclaimed that when He did it, and the world saw it, it would be His indisputable proof to the world that He exists, and He is the only God. This evidence also proves the Bible is the unique Word of God, for it alone records this magnificent prophecy and the proclamation of the proof.

Not only does the Bible record the fulfillment of the prediction, but secular history books also record the geopolitical fulfillment of the *Israel event*. Numerous other books have been written about it. Day by day, radio broadcasts go forth into the entire world declaring the fact of Israel's existence. Israel has now returned to the original land and ever since 1948, has been back upon the world scene. On a regular basis, television news fits in a mention of it. The proof of God's unique and distinctive existence can no longer be denied—except by a fool.

The fool hath said in his heart, There is no God.
—Psalm 14:1

· 14 ·

IS THAT YOUR FINAL ANSWER?

In three words I can sum up everything I've learned about life.
It goes on.
—Robert Frost

W hy are we here? Where did we come from? Where
are we going? Is there a rhyme or reason to our existence? All of these questions are wrapped up in the
ominous inquiry, *"Exactly what is the meaning of life?"* The way
we answer that question is the determiner of how we live the
entirety of our brief lives.

When man attempts to answer these questions apart from an

intelligence or reason behind our existence, he comes up with a bleak, meaningless, and forever-hopeless scenario. When even the remotest possibilities for the reality of God and His purpose for life are omitted from discussion, the absolute *best* that humanity has been able to invent or imagine is the pseudoscientific, conundrum-filled, fatalistic approach to life called *evolution*.

Only three categories of explanation for *how* we arrived here are plausible. One would be that our world has *always* been here. It is eternal. This supposition would declare that life, of some sort, and the universe have always existed.

However, the best scientific evidence we possess, such as the most basic laws of thermodynamics, indicates the opposite: that what we know to be *reality* had a beginning.

The second likelihood is that we are here as the result of the work and plan of an *Intelligent Designer*. At first glance, we find a mound of evidence for this possibility. I admit, this explanation also allows for *alien seeding* and *comet seeding* theories, among other strange and provocative proposals.

As intriguing as these ideas may sound, they do not answer the bigger questions that would beg to be asked. If aliens put us here, from where did *they* arise? If life was seeded by a bombardment of comets containing living microbial ancestors, where, how, and when did these living organisms originate? For this postulation of possibility to make sense at all, we would have to admit that we are here as the result of the purposed design and generated process of an eternally existing Designer (God).

We are now left with the third and final possibility regarding our existence. If we are not here because we have *always* been here, and if we are not here as the result of the purpose of a Designer who exists eternally, then we and all the other millions of life forms are here solely as the result of a cosmic happenstance.

Moreover, this cosmic happenstance conveniently continues

the life cycle of the planet through a mysterious and still *unproven* evolutionary process. To make matters more perplexing, to the best of our current knowledge, *all* of the known life forms in the universe only exist in one place: on *our* planet. We will address this conundrum more thoroughly in the following chapter.

Therefore, if evolution is the answer to life's questions, then in reality, we are left with *more* remarkably complex and, at times, perplexing questions. Evolutionists propose that man is here without the input of an Intelligent Designer. And, they insist there is no reasoned purpose for our presence. We exist simply because of a random, accidental information exchange. To be fair, evolution theory does claim to possess its own definitions of non-accidental processes. Evolution postulation claims it has no need of a necessary intelligence in order to engage in a *purposed* activity of information exchange.

On a regular basis, the evolutionist community uses words like *processes, engaging, purpose,* and *information.* Yet these and other terms, by definition, *require* intelligence behind them when the words are used in their traditional and purest sense.

The majority of *processes,* for example, initiate with intelligent input or manipulation. Inanimate, nonpurposed things do not *engage* in activity without some sort of intelligence or thought process. The word *information* suggests the presence of an intelligent informer and an intelligent recipient. In its traditional sense, the word *information* implies that a message worthy of transmission is on its way and when received will be *understood* by the receiver.

Today's evolutionist finds himself in the awkward position of having to create new definitions for these standard words, and the evolutionists *do* create new definitions. They are masters at the task, but they have to be.

Regardless of the faulty logic, an inescapable fact remains: evolution, and in particular its branch of study called *origins theory*, declares that the *beginning* of everything was a random happenstance, a mere cosmic mishap. Given this scenario, the logical conclusion is that we have no ultimate purpose to life. Life is whatever we make of it. Right and wrong are whatever *we* say they are, whenever we need to make those particular decisions.

Before we continue further, we must point out one of the most obvious and duplicitous double-speaks of evolution postulation. When engaging in a conversation with an evolutionist about the absurdity of abiogenesis or chemosynthesis (spontaneous generation), the evolutionist will frequently say something like this: "Origins theory and evolution are two different things. Evolution only speaks of natural selection and speciation. These things are indisputably proven scientific facts. We do not speak of origins."

Hogwash! Do not be misled nor intimidated by this ruse.

Evolutionists of just a couple decades ago would not attempt to make such a ludicrous argument. They knew that evolution theory begins with and encompasses origins theory. In actuality, they used to be rather proud of the relationship. The two *are* necessarily inclusive of each other.

Many evolution textbooks still used in today's classrooms clearly the inseparable relationship between origins and evolution. I suspect the reason numerous evolutionists of today attempt to separate themselves from current origins theory is that they know (and they know that *we* know) the scientific and foundational underpinnings of origins theory are flawed. Much of it fails even the basic tests of the elementary model of true scientific research.

To deny that evolution has *any* relationship with origins theory would be akin to me saying that I am a believer in Jesus Christ and that He is my Savior and Lord, *but* I do not believe in or espouse the authenticity of the Bible. The Bible is something I ignore in my walk with Jesus. It is not relevant to my discussion regarding my relationship with Jesus.

Obviously, this position would be preposterous because my knowledge of Jesus, in particular His specific claim upon my life as Savior and Lord, comes from the Bible and nowhere else. This absurd position is similar to the argument that numerous evolutionists are taking today. They claim to believe in their *savior* (evolution theory) without believing in or addressing their *bible* (origins theory).

Succinctly stated, the theory of origins insists that all of life arose from a singular source (a common ancestor). This source of life started as the simplest form possible, *and* as a nonliving substance or a conglomeration of nonliving substances (abiogenesis-chemosynthesis).

Once this single-celled life form began more than 600 million *unobserved* years ago, it became a multicelled organism. Evolutionists claim that among the most primitive of the multicelled organisms was the sponge.

The sponge is then declared one of the earliest of the common ancestors to all living things, including the human race. From there, the tale gets worse. It continues to advance itself up the evolutionary ladder. As the ladder continues, it branches off into all the genres of living things known today.

Life goes from the simple to the complex. It proceeds from the sponge (I will skip a few steps here for brevity.) to the worm, to the primordial fish, to the amphibian, and to the reptile. The reptiles split off into three separate branches, from which came dinosaurs, primordial reptilian life, birds, rodents, and in the end, humans.

By the way, humans are declared to have come from the rodent branch of reptilian life. Thus, origins theory's explanation of the arrival of man on planet earth is: *Nonliving matter became a single cell of living matter—by spontaneous generation.*

Funny how something that supposedly evolved from a single-cell organism wound up believing in God! Imagine the consternation of the evolutionist over that final step of the progression of humankind.

All manner of mental gyrations are embarked upon in origins theory—all in the name of rational science. This nonsense is actually taught with a straight face in high schools and universities around the world. People possess PhDs in this pabulum. Governments of the world give tons of money toward research in this so-called *science*. Textbooks are published espousing this to be, in so many words, *the meaning of life*. I kid you not.

Today, origins theory is called modern, enlightened, and scientific knowledge. Aristotle would have been proud.

Did you notice the obvious? What is the undeniable *vehicle* for the origins theory process? What is it that makes origins *work?*

The evolutionary process makes it work. The truth is inescapable. One species of life becomes another species of life through evolution until, in the final analysis, it becomes another *kind* of life—altogether.

Over time, a sponge becomes a rat, eventually becoming a man. Let us not forget that in its original state, the sponge began as some other inanimate substance or substances.

To this day, our classrooms are filled with books, movies, magazines, and scientific journals that espouse origins theory as true and proven science. The majority of them declare that the evolutionary process is the vehicle for *all* of life. In fact, the words *origin* and *evolution* will frequently appear together in the titles of books and other materials. The whole thing is hypocritical to the point of absurdity. Whenever you turn on a television program or pick up a book or magazine that starts with the words *"Billions of years ago . . ."* you are exposed to origins theory. Frequently, it is presented as settled, scientific fact, and it often advances into a discussion of the mystical vehicle of evolution.

The evolutionist who wishes to deny association with origins theory is left with an embarrassing mess on his hands. Evolution proponents will insist that evolution postulation only looks at the ascent of life through the process of speciation and natural selection. They say evolution "does not consider origins theory. "

The problem with this statement is so obvious that the evolutionist hopes you do not see it. The quandary is that no true science deals *only* with a predetermined and one-way process. The evolutionist is not talking about *true science* if he insists on this course of debate.

Can you imagine quantum scientists, for example, saying they are only concerned with how quantum mechanics is observed right now and *not* how it worked from the beginning? Or, on the other hand, would they declare that looking for the *causes* of the observed effects is insignificant? Of course, you cannot imagine this. Yet, the evolutionist wants us to believe that this is how he conducts his science. He wants us to believe that his one-way course of discussion is true and settled science. It is not—not by any real definition of true scientific method.

If evolutionary processes are, in fact, in the continual and current action of evolving life into increasingly complex and varied forms of other life, then it all *had* to have a beginning. In other words, if life is going forward and upward along the evolutionary scale, then we must be able to trace it backwards and downwards as well. When evolution is traced backwards and downwards, it runs into the solid brick wall of *origins*.

Without denial, the two schools of thought connect hand in hand. To say otherwise is to engage in shameless and resolute deceit.

In the evolutionist's fatalistic scenario of how life originated and then progresses, *nothing* must follow this life. We are born, we live, we die, and then we cease. All we have between birth and death is a world full of seeming inconsistencies. We may experience a bit of joy and pleasure, but we will also have pain, death, disease, war, heartache, injustice, and inhumanity. Without a supreme reason, we have no supreme purpose to life, and we have no real answers to the deepest problems of life. Life becomes relegated to the *survival of the fittest* and nothing more.

Furthermore, if we have no supreme purpose or reason, then we do not have supreme morality. Without supreme morality, humans are no different from any other common animal. This is evolution's declaration of life. The evolutionist would insist we are, indeed, no different from a common animal. If that is true, then we have no eternal hope. This certainly is a bleak outlook. Moreover, this is the absolute best creed of life that science has to offer when God is left out of the picture.

Sad to say, much of the world lives by this creed. Why is that? Do they buy into the prevailing scientific *truth* of our day of evolution and evolutionary origins? Of course they do. However, can this really be the *true* meaning to life? Can this be the *true truth* of why we are here and where we are going?

Providentially, this is not the *true truth* of the matter. No *real* scientific, observable, demonstrated, repeatable, falsifiable evidence proves that an evolutionary process, devoid of intelligent input, is the sole origin behind all that we observe as life. This type of real scientific proof does not exist, regardless of the evolutionist's fulminating insistence that it does.

Furthermore, from all we understand, out of the four hundred–plus *known* and discovered planets within our galaxy, ours is the only planet with a singular instance of the presence of life on it. In spite of our desperate and fascinating attempts to find other intelligent life anywhere else in our universe, we have discovered *none,* to date. We have not even discovered a verified microbe. What are the reasonable odds of that if evolution were a scientific fact? Would not this astonishing process of evolution have occurred on at least one other planet somewhere, *anywhere*, in the known universe? A reasonable mind would answer yes. The evolutionist's all-powerful *magical force in the mud* is not so formidable after all.

The next chapter examines the question of the ages: *What is the meaning and purpose of life?* If you would like to know the answer . . . read on.

· 15 ·

THE MEANING OF LIFE

What could be the *purpose* of life? Why *are* we here? Only the Bible, the Word of our Creator, gives us the answers. From Genesis to Revelation, the answer is expounded from several different angles. The Bible's message and the answer to the question of the ages—*What is the meaning and purpose of life?*—are succinctly wrapped up in two remarkable verses:

> Having made known unto us the mystery of his will, according to his good pleasure which he hath purposed in himself: that in the dispensation of the fullness of times he might gather together in one all things in Christ, both which are in heaven, and which are on earth; even in him. (Ephesians 1:9–10)

The apostle Paul wrote this passage to the church at Ephesus, to help these early Christians discern that there is an eternal purpose to life. He wanted them to be certain of the *Grand Scheme*. Further, he wanted them to understand they were a special part of God's grand design. In helping the believers at Ephesus understand this enormous truth, Paul, moved by the Holy Spirit of God, also wrapped up the *entire* biblical message, from cover to cover, regarding the revelation of this ultimate purpose. Here is what Paul declared in these two verses: "Having made known unto us the mystery of his will," is another way of saying, *God has made His plan and purpose for life clear to us. He has revealed it to us through His Word and by His Spirit. We are not in the dark. If we would read His Word from first to last, we would know what God is doing.*

The verse continues by proclaiming, ". . . according to His good pleasure which He hath purposed in Himself: that in the dispensation of the fullness of times . . ." The Word here declares that God's revelation of His will and the accomplishing of His ultimate purpose for life were done at *exactly* the right time, in *exactly* the right way. Thus, in essence, God proclaimed, *I have revealed the answer to the deepest question of life, and I have done it according to My original plan. Now that the plan is complete, it can be clearly seen.* What is this revealed plan? The following words reveal it: *"that He might gather together in one all things in Christ, both which are in heaven, and which are on earth; even in him."*

Bingo! From the beginning in the Garden of Eden, God was working a plan. We are now a part of it. Adam and Eve were a part of it; Satan was a part of it. From eternity past, God purposed to create a kingdom of reality—a huge *fishpond*—that is flawless and in perfect fellowship with Him. This new kingdom will be under the rule and headship of His Son, Jesus Christ.

However, this kingdom is not going to be populated with robots, or puppets on strings, or mere humanoid animals operating by naturalistic instinct. God's perfect kingdom, His real paradise, will be populated by those who know Him, love Him, and follow Him—because they *want* to. What a glorious plan!

Did you notice that this new kingdom would also include beings from the realm of heaven? The verse says that everything in heaven and on Earth will be united under Jesus Christ. The heavenly beings that did not rebel, those who chose by their own free will, are to be included with us in the new kingdom. This new kingdom will ultimately result in a new earth. The Word of God is clear in this matter. Consider the following biblical declarations:

> Nevertheless we, according to his promise, look for new heavens and a new earth, wherein dwelleth righteousness. (2 Peter 3:13)

> And I saw a new heaven and a new earth: for the first heaven and the first earth were passed away; and there was no more sea. (Revelation 21:1)

> For, behold, I create new heavens and a new earth: and the former shall not be remembered, nor come into mind. (Isaiah 65:17)

> For as the new heavens and the new earth, which I will make, shall remain before me . . . (Isaiah 66:22)

Am I suggesting that this life—this world—is not *real*? Of course not. In fact, the opposite is true. To say that this world is not real would be like one fish suggesting to another fish that the fishpond in which they swim is not a reality. However, the truth for us to consider is that *another* reality is coming. The reality in which we now exist will someday cease to exist. The coming, greater reality will be a paradise of perfection. We will no longer experience death, crying, or pain. God will take the old order of things and make it new.

Again, this scenario is like our fishpond illustration. The pond where the fish live, move, breathe, play, eat, and breed is real. The fish are only aware of this particular world. Yet, all along, another world with other life exists in a whole universe about them. The fish are unaware of its existence. They are not equipped to see it nor are they equipped to move within it. Though a greater reality is right outside theirs—they cannot even imagine it. However, their inability to comprehend it does not nullify its existence. It is very real . . . you are living in it.

The apostle John received a foretaste of the greater reality that is to come when he saw a glimpse of our future. Peering for a short while through the surface scum of the *pond*, he saw what is soon to come—God's ultimate plan for the ages. John expressed his *glimpse of glory* in the twenty-first chapter of Revelation:

> And I heard a great voice out of heaven saying, Behold, the tabernacle of God is with men, and He will dwell with them, and they shall be His people, and God Himself shall be with them, and be their God. And God shall wipe away all tears from their eyes; and there shall be no more death, neither sorrow, nor crying, neither shall there be any more pain: for the former things are passed away. And He that sat upon the throne said, Behold, I make all things new. And He said unto me, Write: for these words are true and faithful. And He said unto me, It is done. I am Alpha and Omega, the beginning and the end. I will give unto him that is athirst of the fountain of the water of life freely. He that overcometh shall inherit all things; and I will be His God, and he shall be My son. (vv. 3–7)

Most likely, no one reading this book has ever had a vision like John's. However, if we belong to Jesus in a born-again relationship, I am convinced that we are allowed a *glimpse of glory* every now and then. God has promised it. The glimpses of the coming glory of God come through the Holy Spirit speaking straight to our soul:

> It is written, Eye hath not seen, nor ear heard, neither have entered into the heart of man, the things which God hath prepared for them that love him. But God hath revealed them unto us by his Spirit: for the Spirit searcheth all things, yea, the deep things of God. (1 Corinthians 2:9–10)

Hence, according to the truth revealed in the Word of God, a monumental and supreme purpose and plan for life—your life—exists. God's plan from the beginning was to create a *boot camp*, if you will. This present age is a testing place. It is not a trick, an illusion, or a place of magical manipulation; it is a place of *preparation* for all eternity. According to the Word of God, we will live longer *after* this life than we could ever live *in* this life. That is a thought worth pondering for a while!

God is preparing for Himself a people, but not just any people. He is preparing for Himself a *particular* people. Peter said that we are aliens and strangers in this world:

> Dearly beloved, I beseech you as strangers and pilgrims, abstain from fleshly lusts, which war against the soul. (1 Peter 2:11)

What is the test? What is the thing that God is looking for in His particular and peculiar people? When the atheist or the evolutionist wants to strike out at God, he or she will often say something like, "If there is a God, why is there so much pain and suffering in the world?"

If one is not familiar with God's larger plan, the question

can waylay the Christian. The atheist knows it; as a result, he frequently uses the query. The truth of the matter is this: We have pain and suffering in this world because of man's fallen condition. God allows it to continue as a part of His plan. That is correct. God *planned* for pain and suffering in the world—in that He *knew* man would sin. Of course He knew it. He is God. He is sovereign and omniscient. He is all-knowing. He knew Satan would rebel and tempt His new-formed creation called *humanity*. Actually, God was counting on it.

You may find some of this to be shocking. I assure you it is biblical truth. Remember, man was made to be unlike the animals or any other living thing. He was created in God's image. Man has a free will. He can choose and decide. He can love God or hate Him. He can follow God—or run from Him. He can fellowship with God, or he can reject Him. God knew that man would turn his back on Him, given the right set of circumstances. He also knew that Satan would provide those circumstances.

In much the same way, a drill sergeant knows that a number of recruits will make it, and some will not. Therefore, he applies the pressure. He applies the teaching, the instruction, and the conditions of the new recruit's life. Vigorous training ensues. While in boot camp, recruits will have superb days, wonderful memories formed, and solid experiences to be enjoyed. However, they also endure tough times, trying times, and painful times, often unbearable. Yet, the training marches on.

What is the military trying to accomplish in the final analysis? Do they want all the recruits to be happy? Do they want them to feel satisfied and loved? Do they want every need met for each of the young recruits? No, they want *soldiers*. They want them prepared, equipped, trained, matured, and ready. The ones who survive the test of their own accord and faithfulness to the program qualify to wear the uniform and get to demonstrate and use their attained skills. At any time during the process, they were free to relinquish. However, they did not—they pushed through. Now they are soldiers.

Likewise, but with a much more eternal and glorious goal in mind, God is conducting a boot camp. The test of the ages is now underway, and you are right smack-dab in the middle of it. God is looking for those who will love Him, serve Him, and follow Him, regardless (and *regardless* is a vital word) of what sort of hand this life has dealt them.

We are not left alone in this test. The Lord has demonstrated His love to us. He has given us His Comforter and Guide—His Holy Spirit. He has given us His Church. He has given us each other. He has given us the privilege and gift of prayer and His peace that passes all understanding.

However, the final analysis of this life and this world is not about obtaining supreme happiness or bliss. Ask Job or Jonah or Isaiah or Jeremiah. Ask Peter, James, John, or Paul. Ask *Jesus*. No, this life is the supreme *test*, the boot camp of all boot camps. This life is preparation for the real life to come—the life that lasts forever.

Therefore, when you reach the point in your walk with the Lord where you can say in all honesty that you do not care if He *ever* blesses you again or answers another prayer—you will serve Him *anyway*—then you are well on your way to graduating boot camp.

Job understood this, declared it, and lived it:

Though he slay me, yet will I trust in him." (Job 13:15)

Paul got it, too:

But none of these things move me, neither count I my life dear unto myself, so that I might finish my course with joy, and the ministry, which I have received of the Lord Jesus, to testify the gospel of the grace of God. (Acts 20:24)

Committed to God through thick or thin, Paul taught that

we should live soberly, righteously, and godly, in this present world; looking for that blessed hope, and the glorious appearing of the great God and our Saviour Jesus Christ; who gave himself for us, that he might redeem us from all iniquity, and purify unto himself a peculiar people, zealous of good works. (Titus 2:12–14)

The saints felt the same way, willingly suffering "cruel mock-ings and scourgings, . . . bonds and imprisonment" (Hebrews 11:36)—and more—even though

these all, having obtained a good report through faith, received not the promise: God having provided some better thing for *us*, that they without us should not be made perfect." (vv. 39–40; emphasis added)

While the unbelieving man balls up his fists at God and declares that He is somehow unfair in all of this, the believing soul bows in humility and says, "I will serve you anyway—even if it costs my very life. You have loved me beyond measure."

To that person, the Lord says, *"Well done, My good and faithful servant. Enter now into your new paradise, where I will make all things new, and I will make all things right. You will thank Me for this forever—I assure you."* And the humble servant *will* thank Him—*forever.*

From these passages, we now can understand the larger picture of life. The questions of life are answered for us. Living them out may not be so easy. However, that is not the point. This life was not meant to be easy at every turn. On the contrary, life was meant to be a little tough from time to time, like boot camp.

The questions *are* answered, though. The person who insists on being his own *god* will not like the answers, but they are answered regardless of his preferences.

Where did we come from? We came from the mind and heart of God. Why did He bring us into being? Because He *wanted* to, and because He loved us before we existed. He knew us and loved us before we were formed in our mothers' wombs.

Why are we here? To learn how to love God and each other and to live for God by our own choice, regardless of what life (boot camp) brings our way. Where are we going? To a new, perfect world and a new creation. How long will we be there? *Forever.*

What will we do there? Live—forever! What will life be like there? Life will be real, physical, renewed, perfect, sinless, without death or disease or war or crime and violence. It will be *perfection.* Who may live there? Those who passed the test, who freely surrendered their lives and eternity to Jesus Christ. *Only* those who are covered by His blood sacrifice will live there.

Picture the fish being lifted out of his fishpond, given a new body fitted for a new world, and then allowed to see, live, and experience what was around him all the time—in total perfection, without death, pain, and corruption. The child of God has something parallel to this scenario waiting for him. Maybe this is why Peter was commanded to become a *fisher of men.*

The apostle Peter was given a vision of the new world yet to come. He also saw the temporary nature of this present world. Peter *understood* it—and proclaimed it:

> But the day of the Lord will come as a thief in the night; in which the heavens shall pass away with a great noise, and the elements shall melt with fervent heat, the earth also and the works that are therein shall be burned up. Seeing then that all these things shall be dissolved, what manner of persons

ought ye to be in all holy conversation and godliness, looking
for and hasting unto the coming of the day of God, wherein
the heavens being on fire shall be dissolved, and the elements
shall melt with fervent heat? Nevertheless we, according to
his promise, look for new heavens and a new earth, wherein
dwelleth righteousness. (2 Peter 3:10–13)

Now that you have gained this insight and can see its contextual biblical truth, you understand that we have much work
to do. An immense population is living in the fishpond. Much
of that population does not comprehend the reality of the life
yet to come. They do not see it because they cannot see past the
pond's surface. Nevertheless, *you* can. You can show them the
way. You can speak true truth to them. Now you can do it in
a biblical and competent manner. We are well on our journey
together to that new life—to that new world that is to come. So,
hang on as we unravel the oldest and greatest intrigue known to
humankind—the question of evil.

· 16 ·

THE PROBLEM OF EVIL

What is *cold*? What is *dark*? What, in reality, is the color we call *black?* These three words are our way of describing concepts of reality. We say that we *feel cold,* that the room *is dark*, or that the ink *is black*.

These three words hold something in common. Each can only be measured in the *absence* of something else. This is a profound idea with deep philosophical and biblical meaning.

Let us examine the concept of cold for a moment. Cold can only exist when there is a lack of heat. Heat is the presence of *measurable energy* generated by molecular motion. Cold is only the *lack* of such energy or molecular motion. In the total absence of energy, or heat, coldness is defined. We do not measure cold; temperature is measured in degrees of heat, or energy. When an object is lacking in *degrees*, we then proclaim the object as *cold.*

In a comparable way, the color we call *black* is, in actuality, the absence of true color. Alternatively, it can be defined as the absence of the ability to reflect color and light. The blackness of an object can only be measured by its ability to absorb and reflect light. *Blackness*, then, can be defined as the visual impression experienced when no visible light reaches the eye.

In contrast with brightness, *darkness* is the relative absence of visible light. When light photons are not present, rod and cone cells within the eye are not stimulated. This lack of stimulation means photoreceptor cells are unable to distinguish color frequency and wavelength. When a person enters a dark area, the iris dilates to allow a greater amount of light to enter the eye and thus improve night vision.

The existence of light can be measured. Darkness exists only in its absence and cannot be measured. How can we tell how dark a certain space is? We measure the amount of light that is in it. A singular ray of light can break through complete darkness and illuminate it. A mere lighted match can illuminate a huge space in a dark warehouse.

EVIL OR GOOD?

In the same way that cold, dark, and black only exist in the absence of heat, light, and color, *evil* only exists in the absence of *good.*

The Bible says that God is the ultimate goodness. The Bible, in context, defines this goodness as the holy nature of God (Matthew 19:17). When His overwhelming goodness, or holiness, is absent, or rejected through human choice, evil fills the void. In fact, evil fills the void of morality even to the point of *overwhelming* evil.

To be fair in this analysis of morality and evil, we must point out that the atheist takes a different approach to the same philosophical concept. He uses the same argument that I have made, but then moves it in the opposite direction. At first examination, the atheist's argument appears to present a dilemma for the Christian.

The typical atheist schematic that uses the existence of evil to disprove the existence of the God of the Bible is frequently represented in the following progression:

1. If an all-powerful, perfect, and moral God exists, as is represented in the Bible, then evil cannot exist.

2. The world has evil.

3. Therefore, an all-powerful, perfect, and moral God does not exist.

Modern atheist philosophers have offered further refinements to this argument. At first glance, these added adjustments appear to bolster the atheist's philosophical argument. The enhancements are presented in a scenario such as this:

1. God exists.

2. God is omnipotent, omniscient, perfect, and moral.

3. A perfect and moral being would want to prevent all evil.

4. An omniscient being knows every way evil can come into existence.

5. An omnipotent being who knows every way evil can come into existence has the power to prevent that evil from coming into existence.

6. A being who knows every way an evil can come into existence, and who is able to prevent that evil from coming into existence, and who wants to do so, *would* prevent the existence of that evil.

7. If an omnipotent, omniscient, perfect, and moral being exists, then no evil exists.

8. Evil exists. This is a logical contradiction; therefore, God cannot exist.

THE FATAL FLAW

Each one of these atheistic philosophical schemes possesses the same fatal flaw. Both leave out revealed biblical truths and, thus, the answers to their questions. For the atheist to be fair in this matter, those biblical truths *have* to be considered. After all, the God of the Bible is the One whom the atheist is attempting to disprove. How can one concoct a scheme to disprove the God of the Bible without taking into account what the God of the Bible claims about this same scheme?

Consider the following inquiries: If God were *all-powerful,* would He not also possess the power or ability to withdraw His goodness where it was not desired, wanted, or heeded? Obviously, He would. If He were *all-knowing,* would He not know that withdrawing His goodness or holiness would leave room for evil to work? Again, yes.

If man *was* created with a free will, and God *does* allow man to choose or reject His goodness or holiness, and if by rejecting God's goodness evil *will* fill the void, then how does the presence of evil negate the existence of God? It does not. In fact, this is exactly what God declares about life and about Himself. It is at the heart of God's message in the Bible.

Numbers 3, 5, 6, and 7 in the atheist's argument are fatally flawed since they ignore the revealed truths in the Bible concerning these declarations. Look at these assertions again. My biblical responses follow each of them. My responses are in italics.

3. A perfect and moral being would *want* to prevent all evil.

The Bible declares that God allows evil for His own eternal purpose ("And he hardened Pharaoh's heart, that he hearkened not unto them; as the LORD had said. And the LORD said unto Moses, Pharaoh's heart is hardened, he refuseth to let the people go." [Exodus 7:13–14] Evil, in the end, will be destroyed and not allowed to exist. For the atheist to make this assertion about what God ultimately wants is certainly presumptuous.

5. An omnipotent being, who knows every way an evil can come into existence, has the power to prevent evil from coming into existence.

This is true. The Bible reveals that God does have the power to prevent evil. In fact, this power prevents evil from being unrestrained, in total fashion, at this exact moment. A world with unrestrained evil cannot be imagined by the human mind. Again, the atheist presumes that God wants to totally restrain evil at this time. However, the Bible says that He does not want to restrain evil—yet: "For the mystery of iniquity doth already work: only he who now letteth will let, until he be taken out of the way." (2 Thessalonians 2:7)

6. A being that knows every way an evil can come into existence, who is able to prevent that evil from coming into existence, and who wants to do so, would prevent the existence of that evil.

Again, the Bible is clear that God allows evil (see 1 Peter 1:6–7 and John 9:1–3). To make the statement that God "would want to prevent evil" and "would prevent evil" is another presumption.

7. If an omnipotent, omniscient, perfect, and moral being exists, then no evil exists.

This assertion can be made only if the atheist is the one who determines the circumstances in which God operates (see Genesis 50:20). As a matter of good fortune for us, the atheist is not allowed to call this shot. Again, this is another matter of presumption on the part of the atheist.

Did you notice how often the word *presumption* had to be used in setting the atheist's argument straight? Indeed, atheism is a presumptuous position. This is why the Bible declares the atheist to be a fool. A fool is one who denies or ignores, with calculated purpose, the facts that are before his eyes.

THE GRANDER SCHEME

Life does possess a grander scheme than the mere existence and juxtaposition of goodness and evil. As we discovered in the previous chapter, God is in the process of gathering unto Himself a creation that will love Him and fellowship with Him by free will, regardless of the presence of evil. According to the message of the Bible, God is distinctly using the presence of evil to His eternal glory and our salvation. Rest assured, God has not been fooled.

God did not create evil in the sense that we understand God's

Creation. However, God *knew evil would exist* if His goodness and holiness were muted by man's freedom of will. Evil is only allowed to exist when man freely chooses to reject God's light—and that is precisely what man did:

> And this is the condemnation, that light is come into the world, and men loved darkness rather than light, because their deeds were evil. For every one that doeth evil hateth the light, neither cometh to the light, lest his deeds should be reproved. But he that doeth truth cometh to the light, that his deeds may be made manifest, that they are wrought in God. (John 3:19–21)

Even so, if there were a *complete* absence of light, there would be total darkness. If there were *no* holiness, there would be *absolute* evil. Since the world can be observed to have a measurable mixture of good with evil, then, thankfully, God's goodness has not yet been withdrawn with finality. Sure, the tares are still growing among the wheat, darkness exists with the light, and evil continues to lurk among us—but only because God *allows* it to be so, for the time being. Once the new creation is permeated with God's pure goodness and holiness, evil will no longer abide.

So, the Bible does not claim that because God exists, no evil will exist at all. Instead, it promises that a world without evil *is coming.* That is another predominate message of the Word of God. This is why the Bible states that in the new creation, where God Himself will dwell with humankind, we will have no pain, suffering, sin, death, or evil. In the presence of God's unrestrained and total holiness and goodness, evil cannot exist—it is impossible for it to do so.

The coming kingdom is God's promise to all who believe in Him through Jesus Christ. Hang in there; it will be worth the wait.

IS EVOLUTION
SETTLED SCIENCE?

Without argument, life is filled with *conundrums*. A conundrum is a riddle or a mystery that has yet to be solved. One significant definition of conundrum that is particularly applicable to the direction of this chapter comes from the *Merriam-Webster's 11th Collegiate Dictionary*. The notable definition of the word is the second one; however, I am borrowing, from the first definition, its use of the word *riddle:*

1. a riddle . . .

2. a: a question or a problem having only a *conjectural* answer
   b: an intricate and difficult problem

As we move along, I will prove that evolution theory possesses numerous problems or unanswered riddles associated with it that either have no answers or have only conjectural answers. This fact is significant when examining the veracity of evolution teaching.

Since the evolution supposition is the foundation upon which atheism rests, I must point out how shaky that foundation is, especially if evolution is to be stated as a proven fact. In case an evolutionist objects to my assertion that the theory is presented as *proven* fact, let me verify it.

If evolution is not considered proven fact or at least the best understanding of life that science has to offer, why is it taught *to the exclusion* of all other theories in our public education systems? Why do we so persistently hear or read words such as *"Millions of years ago, our evolutionary ancestors . . ."* or *"Billions of years ago, when the earth was being formed and life was finding its humble beginnings . . ."* as though these statements were irrefutable?

The promoters of evolution teaching use these phrases, and myriads like them, every day. And the statements that begin with such phrases presume that evolution is settled fact. These assertions appear in public school and university textbooks, as well as in science and history television programming and the like. Seldom are qualifying words used when speaking of evolution—such as *theory, supposition, to our best knowledge, or we think.* For the most part, evolution is taught as absolute, established, scientific fact.

Anecdotally, in 2008, the Florida Board of Education made it a legal *requirement* for evolution to be taught in the public education classrooms. The updated Florida guidelines state,

"The scientific theory of evolution is the fundamental concept underlying all of biology."[1]

A number of textbooks make the categorical claim that evolution has been proved and verified by science. So to say that evolution is not presented and taught as fact in many official venues is simply not an honest statement.

My thesis is this: Evolution theory, while it does offer numerous fascinating suppositions and has stated some *true truth* along the way, is *far* from being settled science. Too many unanswered questions remain. They are not little ones either; they are monumental ones. They are conundrums of deep significance.

Before we examine several conundrums of evolution theory, let me be fair about this. Simply because a scientific notion possesses unanswered questions does not always render that notion *unscientific*. Furthermore, unanswered questions do not render it disqualified from debate or further scientific and philosophical exploration.

The law of gravity is a superb illustration of this fact. While we accept its premise as scientific reality, there is still much about gravity that we do not understand. Several theories still exist as to what gravity is and what makes it work. The same line of reasoning would follow for quantum mechanics research.

We must also emphasize that for almost every conundrum I will present, evolution has a theory as to its possible answer. I must also add that in each case their theories are mere *conjectures*. Several of their conjectural theories are outlandish, not only in my opinion but also in those of several noteworthy and credible scientists. A number of the conjectures proffered are not adequate in their scientific explanation. This does not mean they are false or that they hold no merit. This lack of scientific information does mean that conjecture alone cannot prop up a conundrum. It means the problem cannot be ignored so the greater theory can be declared as an incontestable scientific fact. Again, this is not honest or acceptable science.

Deep conundrums exist which evolution theory has yet to answer. Proffering a theory that has unanswered questions is a legitimate part of the scientific method. However, as you will see, a number of these unanswered evolutionary mysteries are so deep, so profound, and so foundational that to not have the answers to them denotes that we are not yet ready to speak of evolution theory as the answer to how life arrived here. Therefore, evolution should not be set forth as though it were established, scientific fact to the exclusion of all other possibilities.

Since the vast majority of evolution teaching *does*, without refute, present itself as settled, scientific fact—to the exclusion of all other possibilities—I am proposing that much of evolution teaching today is not honest science. I do not propose that *everything* evolution teaches is false. Nor have I ever proposed that evolution theory should not be taught at all—as *theory*. After all, the theory of evolution is a predominant theory and the foundational underpinning of a major worldview. If a person is going to be educated in the realities of life and the various views to which people of all cultures hold, then it makes sense that in order to receive a decent education, he or she should be taught all the reasonable theories.

If, however, one is taught only a singular theory, to the exclusion of all others, and if he is taught that this one *theory* is confirmed scientific fact, regardless of the copious amount of conundrums it contains, it is no longer an education he is receiving—it is *indoctrination*.

On the other hand, in the preponderance of Christian schools and/or home school coursework, the students are taught the in-depth proposals of evolution theory along with the theories of Creation and Intelligent Design. Rather than being indoctrinated, the student who is taught both theories of origins and life is receiving an honest *education*.

What are the mysterious conundrums of which I speak? I will present several examples of some of the foundational questions evolution has not yet been able to answer. These questions are so fundamental that to be unable to answer them with scientific integrity reduces evolution theory to the category of *attractive theory,* but not *established fact.* Consider the detailed examples in the next chapter, and see if you do not agree.

· 18 ·

PONDERING PESKY PUZZLES

Scientists now understand that the universe in which we live is comparable to a precision-designed instrument of unimaginable magnitude. In fact, the universe appears tweaked to a point of absolute precision for the sole purpose of enabling life on earth.

We live on a planet with scores of improbable, interdependent, and life-supporting conditions that make it a tiny oasis in an enormous and hostile universe. The scope of the universe's fine-tuning makes the *anthropic principle* perhaps one of the most powerful arguments for the existence of an Intelligent Designer. These precise and interdependent environmental conditions, called *anthropic constants*, make up what is known as the *anthropic principle*.

The word *anthropic* comes from the Greek word that means "human" or "man." Thus, *anthropology* is the study of the origin and social relationships of the human being.

The *anthropic principle* is merely a fancy title that expresses the burgeoning evidence that has a number of modern scientists believing the universe is finely tuned (designed) for the specific purpose of supporting human life. More than one hundred cataloged and narrowly defined constants point to the possibility of an Intelligent Designer.

These constants include such things as our exacting distance from the sun, the meticulous balance of gravitational forces, the earth's axis rotation rate, and the thickness of the earth's crust. They also include the preciseness of atmospheric discharge, the delicate balance of the thickness of our protective and life-sustaining atmosphere, and the interaction of the salt and freshwater bodies. In addition, the list includes the necessity of specific types of vegetation, the precise chemical balances of the air we breathe, and the absolute necessity of the interconnectivity of our ecology, from honey bees to rain forests.

Without these precise, measured, and necessary balances, along with scores and scores of others with equal importance, we would not . . . we *could not* . . . be here. I have only named about a dozen of these constants. As stated before, scientists have cataloged more than a hundred anthropic constants.

Credible scientists have calculated the staggering improbability that these more than one hundred–plus cataloged constants would exist today for *any* planet in the universe merely by chance. Several statistical formulas put the probabilities in the range of 1 chance in 10 to the 138th power.*

To understand how large this number is, consider that only about 10 to the 70th power atoms exist in the *entire* universe. In other words, we have a 0 percent chance that *any* planet in the universe would have all of the life-supporting conditions that we have. This mathematical fact almost stands alone in demanding that an Intelligent Designer is behind our anthropic-friendly planet.

From our understanding of the anthropic principle, we can further theorize that the exacting conditions conducive for life must be *uncommon* in the remainder of what we know about our universe. This would be true for intelligent life of a high order as well as the simplest of animal life. Any such life would be exceptional in our galaxy and in the entire universe. This scientific and startling information has led several former skeptics to the recent conclusion that *"maybe we are alone in the universe, after all."*

Consider the following excerpt from a *New York Times* Science Review article.[1] The article reviewed a book entitled *Rare Earth: Why Complex Life Is Uncommon in the Universe*.[2] In this book, Peter Ward, professor of geological sciences and curator of paleontology at the University of Washington, and Donald Brownlee, professor of astronomy at the University of Washington, surveyed the circumstances that are essential for life to materialize. The *New York Times* review of the book reveals a shocking admission by these two prominent scientists.

> Drawing on new findings in astronomy, geology and paleontology, the two argue that humans might be alone, at least in the stellar neighborhood, and perhaps in the entire cosmos.

---

*Dr. Hugh Ross is one such scientist to calculate this probability. He has a PhD in astronomy and astrophysics. He has written or collaborated on more than a dozen books and fifty scientific articles. He is the founder of a ministry called Reasons To Believe.

They say modern science is showing that Earth's composition and stability are extraordinarily rare. Most everywhere else, the radiation levels are too high, the right chemical elements too rare in abundance, the hospitable planets too few in number and the rain of killer rocks too intense for life ever to have evolved into advanced communities.[3]

Consider this comparable quote from Dr. Michael Denton, senior research fellow in human molecular genetics at the University of Otago in New Zealand. Here he summarizes the evidence that he says exists for "a finely-tuned universe."

No other theory or concept imagined by man can equal in boldness and audacity this great claim that all the starry heavens, and every species of life, that every characteristic of reality exists for mankind. But most remarkably, given its audacity, it is a claim which is very far from discredited pre-scientific myth. In fact no observation has ever laid the presumption to rest. And today, four centuries after the scientific revolution, the doctrine is again reemerging. In the last decades of the twentieth century, its credibility is being enhanced by discoveries in several branches of fundamental science.[4]

While not every scientist in the world would agree with these conclusions, the evidence for this stated postulation is mounting. Hence, if we are alone in the universe and all the latest evidence supports this claim, then *why* are we alone? Why does Earth alone support our life? In addition, Earth does not merely support *our* life; our planet supports *all* known life within the entirety of the universe. The several million species of known life seem to exist in only one place in the entire universe—planet Earth.

Consider this: What would happen if all the saltwater systems were removed from our earth? In time, we would die. What if all the freshwater sources were removed? The answer is the same. What if all the animals were removed or if all the insects were gone or if all the plant life disappeared? Again, we would eventually die.

Now think about this: What if humans and only humans were removed from the planet? Everything would continue. The ecology is perfect. The system would sustain itself without us.

The evidence would appear, then, that humans are not here for the earth, but the earth is here for humans and humans alone. On top of that, only the earth and no other known place in the universe can sustain the human race.

Again, scientific mystery in and of itself does not disprove evolution as a possibility. However, it certainly does reduce evolution to a category much less than a proven, scientific, undeniable fact. Neither does the anthropic principle, beyond all doubt, prove that creationism is the undeniable truth. Nevertheless, it gives more credence to a biblical worldview than the secular, evolutionary worldview.

These incredible and precise numerical values required for life confront scientists with obvious and difficult implications. The remarkable fact is that the values of these anthropic constants seem to be adjusted with such precision as to make possible not only the development but also the sustaining of life, only here on our earth.

The reality is that we live on a unique planet. We are perfectly positioned in an extraordinary solar system that is ideally located in an enormous and rare galaxy that exists within a remarkable and implausible universe. Yet, the message of the Bible alone implies that we are indeed the crowning glory of the universe. We are the center of God's heart. We are the ones for whom God sent His Son to die for our sins. We are the ones to whom God reaches out His hand of forgiveness and reconciliation. Our life *does* have purpose, value, and meaning.

THE IMPROBABLE NECESSITY FOR FOOD

DNA (deoxyribonucleic acid) molecules in plants, humans, and all living things are all the same shape. The shape is comparable to a twisted ladder or a double helix. The backbone of the ladder is made up of sugar and phosphate molecules. The DNA molecules, together with their unique information transfer system of RNA (ribonucleic acid), are the foundational building blocks of life—all of life.

Each rung on the ladder of DNA is made up of two bases that stick out from the backbone and then pair in the middle. This pairing is called a *base pair*. The letters *A*, *T*, *G*, and *C* represent the chemical names of these bases. The twisted ladder forms the unique DNA molecule shape of which we are so familiar. DNA is folded, stored, copied, and used as a blueprint to make proteins. This process is accomplished in the same way in all living things.

RNA is equally vital to DNA, even if it is lesser known. RNA is significant because it plays a critical role in helping DNA copy and express genes and to transport genetic material within the cell. RNA also serves a number of other independent functions that are central to the sustaining of life within the cell.

DNA plays a crucial role in the production of RNA. In essence, DNA contains the *blueprints* for making RNA. Therefore, when the cell requires more RNA, it pulls up the necessary information in the DNA and gets to work making more RNA. This process is known as *transcription*, alluding to the fact that the information is copied from one molecule to another.

It is a scientific fact that the instructions for almost all living things come from DNA. Functions that are unique to a plant or animal have unique proteins, but proteins that do the same things in numerous organisms have parallel instructions or DNA sequences.

Thus, if all living things hold in common the same basic

structures or building blocks for life, why are all living things so different? A number of the differences come from the order of As, Ts, Cs, and Gs and the proteins they code. The differences can also be the result of the time and place these proteins are made. Furthermore, the variations in living things are the result of the number of chromosomes and genes contained within the genome.

Plant and animal cells perform several of the same functions. The genes involved in these functions have comparable sequences. One of these functions is called *cellular respiration*; that is, the process that converts sugar and oxygen to water and carbon dioxide—to make energy for the cell. In order for this process to take place, we have to eat.

When we ingest other living things, the DNA of those living things (fruits, vegetables, nuts, meats, etc.) just happens to be compatible with our DNA so that cellular respiration can take place. If it were not for the fact that our DNA is so akin to all other living things, we could not eat. If we could not eat, we would die.

Is the process of eating and cellular respiration the result of a mere fluke of evolution? Alternatively, could it be that a common Designer made certain that the process of eating and cellular respiration would function in such a precise and perfect manner? Which answer appears to be the most probable to you?

If the supposed cosmic and random happenstance of evolution was the real reason that all living things exist, why, when, and how did this happenstance mechanism decide that living things *needed* to eat anything in the first place? Would it not be odd that evolution should come up with the idea of food and energy creation through cellular respiration? Cellular respiration is an astoundingly complex, energy-expending system.

Yet in order for life to be sustained, living things must have other living things to ingest. What an odd thing for a mere cosmic *coincidence* to develop, by random generation. Is it not a strange convenience for evolution that all living things have such unimaginable DNA similarity that cellular respiration is possible?

Evolution supposition leaves us, then, with several puzzling conundrums:

- *When* did the need to eat other living things originate?

- *Why* did the need to eat other living things originate?

- *How* did the need to eat other living things originate?

- Why would natural selection not have chosen or produced a much simpler and more energy-efficient solution for the energy needs of a living organism?

- Why would natural selection not have chosen a much more ecology-friendly solution for the sustenance of life for its several million species?

THE IMPROBABLE UNIQUENESS OF MAN

Out of the myriads of species of life on planet Earth, humans stand uniquely beyond all the others. Let us remember our discussion in chapter 7 when we were looking at the technical definition of man as being "created in God's image." We discovered this meant that man is indescribable in his difference from anything else in all of creation. God declared that nothing in all creation was analogous to humankind.

Undoubtedly, animals such as the great apes, chimps, and monkeys resemble our appearance and can even mimic human mannerisms. Even so, the smartest of apes does not come close in comparison with a human toddler in overall intelligence and in the toddler's innate world-changing capabilities.

The majority of evolutionists agree that the chimpanzee is the most intelligent life on the planet, next to humans. Evolutionists are giddy in presenting the numerous similarities between chimps and humans. They will, in short order, point out the chimp's ability to perform basic communication techniques and their antiquated use of elementary *weapons* (throwing rocks).

The real difference between a human and a chimp is comparable to the difference that exists between a chimp and a lone rock lying in the bottom of a secluded valley. Evolutionists conveniently ignore the fact that chimps and humans are a universe apart in a myriad of undeniable ways.

Do chimps and humans look alike in several slight ways? Yes, we do. Do we commonly possess much of the same DNA structure? Yes, we do. A number of scientists say we share as much as 98 percent similarities. The latest reliable research, available at the time of this book's writing, however, indicates the DNA similarity between man and chimps is much closer to 94 percent. The genome similarity, logically, would explain why we look slightly alike, but that is about where the real comparisons end—though this 94 to 98 percent range is given as *proof* of an imagined evolutionary process that connects chimps and man through a mysterious (yet-undiscovered) common ancestor!

Given the universe of difference between a chimp and a human, is it not interesting that only a 2 to 4 percent difference in DNA structure could produce such a superior race of species as is observed in humankind? Much more scientific sense is made to at least consider the possibility that the reason a chimp and a man have such similarity in overall genome structure is that we have a common Creator who used common building blocks.

It is also worth noting that a large number of evolutionists will leave out the scientific fact that *all living things* hold in common numerous DNA traits with every other living thing.

When they do mention this startling fact, they do so in an attempt to prove that we *must* have come from a common ancestor. I suppose the possibility never crosses their minds that the commonalities could just as well indicate a common Creator. More than likely, the reason for this is that, even though much evidence is before them, from the beginning, they launch their research from a secular worldview. Remember from the outset, this worldview claims no *need* for an Intelligent Designer.

Modern researchers have discovered astonishing DNA structural resemblances between extremely simple organisms and human beings. It is hard enough to accept that little creatures such as worms and flies are so comparable to us in genome structure, but we have also discovered only of late that human DNA is also comparable to baker's yeast in several remarkable ways.

What, you might ask, do we have in common with baker's yeast, which is in reality just a common fungus? The answer is astonishing.

We are so parallel to yeast in a number of our genes that human DNA can be successfully substituted for an equivalent yeast gene. This was first demonstrated in 1985 when researchers at Cold Spring Harbor Laboratory "rescued" a mutant yeast cell that lacked an essential developmental gene. They accomplished this remarkable feat by inserting the human gene into the cell. This "remarkable result," wrote David Botstein, a yeast researcher at Stanford, "indicated a profound conservation not only of [DNA] sequence but also of detailed biological function" over at least a billion years of evolution from yeast to human. "More than 70 additional human genes have proved able to repair various mutations in yeast," he said. Botstein's conclusion was: "What is true for yeast is also true for humans."[5]

Nonetheless, neither a yeast cell nor a chimp comes close to a human in scores of incontrovertible and obvious ways. In fact, *nothing* out of the many millions of species on the earth comes within several universes of proximity to the complexity of the human being.

For instance, human beings are the only species . . .

to display a complex consciousness (making us capable of abstract reasoning, introspection, extremely advanced and complex problem solving, and generating and sharing thoughts, ideas, words, and literature);

to advance almost limitless technology (what the human mind can conceive, it can, in all probability, invent, produce, and use);

to build complex societies with laws, courts, rules, and written codes of multifaceted regulations;

to build prisons in order to separate certain members of our society from the rest;

to build complex buildings for shelter, which we then arrange into communities and sprawling cities with interconnecting, complex, technological infrastructures;

to transport and mobilize through artificial means of technologically produced transportation vehicles;

to invent technologies that travel underwater, through the air, and into space;

to display morals and moral judgments to hold other society members accountable;

to use complex language forms—spoken, written, and signed with our hands and body motions;

to invent artificial technological language forms, such as the various types of computer languages;

to invent more than six thousand unique language *types* within our own singular species;

to produce written, generational knowledge fashioned in a specific manner for generational transference;

to build libraries, write books, and invent computers that store our generational knowledge;

to produce and wear clothing;

to discover and use various mathematical principles and apply them to the invention of numerous technologies;

to invent the art of tool crafting, manufacturing, and use;

to seek to control and manipulate the environment in which we live (we are the only species that is remotely capable of manipulating our environment);

to build temples and altars and to worship, both as individuals and as a corporate community;

to build fires and construct artificial fire-making devices;

to farm and grow food for our own species and to provide it for numerous other species;

to cook food;

to produce medicines and provide medical assistance for each other as well as the animal life around us;

to perform surgery;

to care for all the other species of the world in a concerted effort;

to build weapons of war and assemble in military units to wage war against entire societies; and

to build zoos where we contain and study examples of the other life around us.

The list goes on and on, but certainly you understand the point. We are different in a myriad of indescribable ways. We are as "gods" to the rest of the planet. As far as we know, nothing on the planet or in the entire universe compares with the human being. Nothing comes within a cosmos of closeness. The chimp, the dog, the dolphin, and the whale are intelligent and astonishing creatures. However, none of these animals comes remotely close to the intelligence and the world-changing potential of a single two-year-old human child.

The scientific conclusion that makes the most logical sense is that humans are the result of intelligent design. An Intelligent Designer specifically elevated us to a level that is a *universe of difference* above every other living thing in the world. Without a doubt, we alone are tasked with dominion over all the earth. Observably, and without debate, that is the way it is, whether the evolutionists like it or not.

This is what the Bible has been declaring for more than three thousand years. Moreover, according to actual science, the biblical declaration makes sense as well. Does the theory that man evolved from a chimp through a common ancestor make any sense at all? Scientifically speaking, no, it does not.

The absolute uniqueness of man is indeed an embarrassing conundrum for the evolutionist who desires to relegate man to a mere evolutionary branch off the one huge tree. The branch of *humankind* simply does not fit with the rest of the tree.

One more thing to ponder in this line of discussion: humans are the only species capable of *thinking* about such things! If our brains are merely the result of an evolutionary process, first brought about by random happenstance within a primordial soup billions upon billions of years ago, how can we trust our evolved thought processes to lead us into rational considerations about who we are and from where we came?

If evolution is the answer to the existence of our brains and thought processes, why are we the *only* species capable of such thought? Why are we the only ones who communicate about it, write about it, debate about it, and then pass on our generational knowledge about the possible means of our own origins? What a conundrum!

THE AMAZING HUMAN BODY AND ITS SYSTEMS

The human body has at least eleven main systems operating in exacting and life-sustaining concert. These systems are categorized as follows:

- circulatory
- respiratory
- immune
- skeletal
- excretory
- muscular
- endocrine (hormone regulation)
- digestive
- nervous
- integumentary (skin, hair, nails, etc.)
- reproductive

Each of these astounding and intricate systems is made up of copious smaller parts. Each part serves a unique function. These parts are constructed of countless microscopic cells. Many of these cells are unique from all the other cells of the body.

Each cell ensures that the small parts of the systems, and the systems as a whole, function properly. With the exception of the reproductive system, if even one of these systems shuts down, you will die. These systems must be in place and fully functioning in order for your body to live. In reality, then, the human body is made up of systems within systems within systems. The intricacy is astounding and unfathomable.

If all living organisms, including humans, arrived here in their present form by chance, then how do we explain the presence of such complex, interwoven and multiple systems that are so necessary to each other's survival? How did it come about that each system is made of copious parts and unique cells with unique functions working in concert with one another? If there is an obvious necessity for all the systems to be in one accord for us to live, would this not mean, in a logical sense, that they had to first appear together, at the same time, and working in perfect accord? Is it probable that the systems would have appeared at the same time, working in perfect unity, through the unpurposed evolutionary process? If not, is it probable that each one formed in a mysterious evolutionary sequence that was separated by millions of years? If this is the case, then why, how, and when did these systems begin to *know* that each of them *needed* another in order to function properly? Again, *why* would they make such a determination?

Evolutionists say that living things look for efficiency as they randomly seek their own survival, purpose, and function. If this is factual, then why would the human body seek to make itself more complicated, only to ensure the increase of the odds of its ultimate demise by losing a vital system to disease or accident?

Moreover, *how* would it accomplish this? What are the odds that *one* intricate system, filled with its own mysterious and complex wonders of unique and interworking cells and subsystems, would have evolved through a random process? Why would the singular system have evolved only to somehow determine that it *needed* to add yet another system, and then another, and another, and another, and another?

When did this evolving organism decide that enough was enough? *Why* did it decide that enough was enough? *How* did it decide? Are systems still evolving within our own bodies? If this is true, where is the evidence? If this statement is *not* true, why not? Has the evolution process stopped? If evolution of our body systems has stopped, then does that not belie the meaning of the word *evolution*?

When one considers the following additional facts, the idea of random natural selection, origins theory, and evolution grow more absurd.

- Every square inch of the human body has about 19 million skin cells.

- Every hour about 1 billion cells in the human body must be replaced.

- The circulatory system of arteries, veins, and capillaries in your body is about 60,000 miles long.

- The heart has to beat more than 2.5 billion times in an average lifetime in order to sustain the human body.

- Humans have about 9,000 taste buds on the surface of the tongue, in the throat, and on the roof of the mouth.

- The proper function of the eye requires that you blink more than 10,000,000 times a year.

Endlessly they continue, the unfathomable intricacies of the systems, cells, and functions of the human body. How can an unpurposed process that began in a primordial soup millions of years ago without intelligent input explain these intricate details? I argue that they cannot be explained by mere evolution theory to the *exclusion* of all other theories.

When examined from a scientific standpoint, it would appear that we are created in a wonderful way. In a more logical sense, life was purposed by an Intelligent Designer. Creation itself declares His glory and power.

However, according to evolution postulation, your life is a mere random whim of several billion cells, intricately working together in perfect synchronization, and they just happen to be bound and determined, on their own, to be uniquely *you*! This is an unthinkable conundrum indeed.

NOW, LET US TALK ABOUT SEX!

Few books these days are considered "marketable" unless they include *sex* in them. Consequently, this book will include a little sex within its pages.

Questions: How did all of humankind originate at the *same* time, but with separate sexual systems fully operating, ready to work as functioning *males* and *females*? Why, when, and how did these two sexes originate?

Evolutionist Dr. Graham Bell, in his book *The Masterpiece of Nature: The Evolution of Genetics and Sexuality*, describes the sexuality conundrum this way:

> Sex is the queen of problems in evolutionary biology. Perhaps no other natural phenomenon has aroused so much interest; certainly none has sowed as much confusion. The insights of Darwin and Mendel, which have illuminated so many mysteries, have so far failed to shed more than a dim and

wavering light on the central mystery of sexuality, empha-
sizing its obscurity by its very isolation.[6]

To be fair to Dr. Bell, he does discuss in his book his hypothesis as to how the sexes might have originated. However, we can
make several observations about his discussions. First, he admits
in the preceding statement that in spite of his theory or any other
such theory, sex is still the "queen of problems in evolutionary
biology." Second is the fact that different evolutionists give dif-
fering answers to this same perplexing riddle. The fact is that
evolution has yet to agree on an answer as to how this remarkable
thing called sex could have happened. Yes, this is the queen of
evolution conundrums.

In an article in *Bioscience*, titled, "How Did Sex Come
About?" author Julie Schecter wrote:

> Sex (obviously occurs everywhere in nature) . . . Yet sex
> remains a mystery to researchers . . . Why sex? Sex takes
> much longer and requires more energy than simple cell divi-
> sion. Why did a process so blatantly unprofitable to its earliest
> practitioners become so widespread?[7]

The evolution of sex and its accompanying capability of
reproduction is not a preferred topic of debate among the
majority of evolutionists. No matter the numerous theories they
invent, they still must cross the inescapable obstacle concerning
the origin and the purpose of the first fully functional female and
the first fully functional male. While various evolutionary theories
attempt to explain why sex exists *now*, they do not and cannot
explain the origin of sex. Sex is a true evolutionary puzzlement.

Moreover, biology textbooks, on the topic of origins, consistently illustrate amoebas evolving into various intermediate organisms, which then evolve into amphibians, reptiles, mammals, and

eventually humans. Yet, we are not told at exactly which point the independent male and female sexes originated. This part of the tale is conveniently left out. Perhaps there may be a nefarious reason why this part of the tale is missing.

The truth is that somewhere along this supposed evolutionary pathway, both the male and female genders were required to ensure the further existence of a particular species. How do evolutionists explain this? They do not know with any degree of certainty. The multitudes of evolutionary theories that abound are evidence that the secular scientific community does not have a clue how to answer this question.

How could nature have randomly evolved a female member of a species that produces eggs and is internally equipped to nourish a growing embryo? At the same time, how did nature randomness evolve a male member of the species that produced sperm cells able to mobilize themselves within the reproductive organs of the female until they united with the egg? How did these cells, egg and sperm, conveniently evolve to ensure that each contained half the normal chromosome number necessary to produce the cells of the completed organism? Renowned evolutionist Philip Kitcher has noted that "despite some ingenious suggestions by orthodox Darwinians, there is no convincing Darwinian history for the emergence of sexual reproduction."[8]

Evolutionists continue to admit that the origin of gender and sexual reproduction remains one of the most difficult problems in biology when viewed from a purely evolutionary model.

In his book, *The Cooperative Gene*, evolutionist Mark Ridley wrote: "Evolutionary biologists are much teased for their obsession with why sex exists. Sex is a puzzle that has not yet been solved; no one knows why it exists."[9]

What I am going to say next is an extremely important point to emphasize. None of the preceding material is meant to suggest that we now have conclusive evidence that evolution is a complete impossibility. Because I approach life from a distinctly biblical worldview, I do not believe that evolution is the vehicle whereby life, and in particular humankind, arrived on earth. In this regard, I believe the Creation account of the first several chapters of Genesis.

My discourse in this chapter has been to present only several of the numerous and overwhelming conundrums that perplex the theory of evolution. I do this to illustrate my first point; evolution is *not* a settled, scientific, foregone conclusion. Evolution may propose several fascinating and provocative theories and postulations, but it cannot and should not be proclaimed as *settled science.*

Let me repeat: *Evolution is not a settled fact, no matter at what volume the ardent evolutionist screams that it is.* The Christian has no need to be intimidated by the atheist and/or the evolutionist who attempts to assert that evolution is settled science. It is not. It is fascinating speculation, but it is not *settled* science.

Following are several more examples of mysteries for which evolutionists have no plausible explanations. Evolution theorists do not know:

- how matter originated

- why matter originated

- when matter originated

- how the universe began

- why the universe began

- when the universe began

- how the solar system formed

- why the solar system formed

- when the solar system formed

- how the first living cell came into being

- why the first living cell came into being

- when the first living cell came into being

- how nonlife became life

- why nonlife became life

- when nonlife became life

- how the first single cell became a multicell

- why the first single cell became a multicell

- when the first single cell became a multicell

- how DNA/RNA originated

- why DNA/RNA originated

- when DNA/RNA originated

- how DNA/RNA can exhibit such a complex language with no original and apparent reason to do so

- where water came from

- why 70 percent coverage of liquid water on a planet is only located on *our* planet

- why the fossil records do not scientifically demonstrate an evolutionary chain

- where the common ancestor for man and chimp is located on the evolutionary chain

- why humans alone rule all the other species of the earth

Again, I give these not as evidence to disprove evolution, for evolutionists *do* from time to time offer various answers to the majority of these questions. The point is that they do not conclusively agree on the answers, because they do not *know* the answers with any degree of certainty. Again, not knowing answers to a scientific theory does not necessarily make it unscientific or untrue. What it *does* say is this: *when a large number of foundational questions exist that cannot be answered concerning a particular scientific theory, it becomes more probable that the theory cannot be declared as settled science.*

Clearly, the theory of evolution has too many unanswered *foundational* questions that beg to be settled with scientific answers if it hopes to be proclaimed as settled, scientific, and irrefutable *fact*. It follows somewhat naturally that there are too many unanswered foundational questions for evolution theory to be *exclusively* taught in our public education systems.

If only one or two unanswered questions existed, it would be a different matter. The same would be true if the unanswered questions did not go to the foundational underpinnings of the theory. However, as I have just illustrated, numerous conundrums go to the very foundation of evolutionary understanding and suppositions. If evolution wants to set itself up as the absolute and irrefutable scientific explanation for the origins and continuation of the species, it will need to do better than it has done thus far.

I suspect that evolution has not been set up by the world system because of its settled scientific nature. It has been clearly demonstrated that it is far from settled science. I propose that it has been set up precisely because it is the only answer—the only *substitute*—that comes close to satisfying the secular (godless) worldview's questions of life. It has been chosen specifically for this reason and this reason alone. Overall, evolution has done an extremely poor job as a substitute.

> Finally, my brethren, be strong in the Lord, and in the power of His might. Put on the whole armour of God, that ye may be able to stand against the wiles of the devil. For we wrestle not against flesh and blood, but against principalities, against powers, against the rulers of the darkness of this world, against spiritual wickedness in high places. Wherefore take unto you the whole armor of God, that ye may be able to withstand in the evil day, and having done all, to stand. (Ephesians 6:10–13)

I pray this book will help you to stand.

· 19 ·

BUT THEY HAVE
NEVER HEARD!

God's fairness is not limited by our failures.

Crowley, the atheist antagonist from chapter 1, brought
up a classic argument that often throws Christians
for a loop: *What about those who have never heard the
gospel?* At first consideration, this challenge appears daunting.
It can be debilitating to the unprepared Christian, but it does
not have to be.

Typically, the biblical antagonist will state the challenge

something like: "If you claim that the Christian faith and belief in Jesus Christ is the only way for anyone to be saved, what about the people who have never heard your gospel or have never been given the chance to hear a preacher or sit in a church? What about those who have never heard of a Bible or heard the name Jesus? If no one can be saved apart from hearing about and believing upon Jesus, then just how fair is your God?"

These are honest questions; they are fair questions. However, they initiate from an unbiblical understanding of life. The biblical worldview filters all questions and observations through the revealed truth of the Word of God. The Bible has the answers to all of these questions.

Of course, a person is not guaranteed that he or she will necessarily appreciate the answers, but the answers *are* there, and they *are* clear. Several are revealed in direct biblical statements. Others are gleaned from the principles, conclusions, and overall contextual teachings of God's Word.

When secularists ask the question, "What about those who have never heard?" they frequently assume things that are not biblically accurate. Let us examine these false conjectures. We have at least three significant ones to analyze.

THE FIRST FALSE ASSUMPTION: MAN IS UNKNOWING

The first secular assumption is that humanity is somehow ignorant of the existence of God and our subsequent accountability to Him. If you have stuck with me thus far, you understand by now that I do not believe this is the case at all.

I believe that humankind knows God exists, and that we know something of His moral law because He has placed this truth in our hearts, and it binds us to Him. A particular person may not yet know the truth of Jesus Christ and the gospel message, but he knows of God and of our eternal accountability to Him. The Bible straightforwardly addresses this universal truth in at least two prominent passages of Scripture.

> He hath made every thing beautiful in his time: also he hath set the world [eternity] in their heart, so that no man can find out the work that God maketh from the beginning to the end. (Ecclesiastes 3:11)

> That which may be known of God is manifest in them [men]; for God hath shewed it unto them. For the invisible things of him from the creation of the world are clearly seen, being understood by the things that are made, even his eternal power and Godhead; so that they are without excuse: because that, when they knew God, they glorified him not as God, neither were thankful; but became vain in their imaginations, and their foolish heart was darkened. (Romans 1:19–21)

The Bible could not be clearer on this point. We are without excuse in this matter. No one can stand before God and say, "I didn't know that You existed." The protestation might pass for an excuse in a university or a high school classroom or in a debate, but it will not fly with God. His Word is clear.

We are not without knowledge, and we are accountable for what we know about God. God will sort out the rest from there. He is more than capable to render a righteous judgment in this matter.

Christians are charged with delivering the truth of God's Word and the gospel of Jesus Christ to as many as God directs us. However, even if Christians fail to deliver the message, still no one can ever say to the Lord, "I did not know."

The fact that all humanity *does know* about God, yet a number of them willfully choose to deny His authority over their lives, leads us to the second false assumption in this eternal matter.

THE SECOND FALSE ASSUMPTION: MAN IS WITHOUT GUILT

The second false assumption is that man is *innocent* from the beginning rather than *guilty* from the beginning. This truth calls for an explanation.

When someone asks, "What of those who have never heard?" that individual presupposes that people are walking around the planet in *innocence*, without a sin nature that has condemned them already. If they are innocent and God condemns them to hell only because they did not hear and respond to a specific message, then He *would* be unfair. However, such is not the case.

> He that believeth on him is not condemned: but he that believeth not is condemned already, because he hath not believed in the name of the only begotten Son of God. And this is the condemnation, that light is come into the world, and men loved darkness rather than light, because their deeds were evil. (John 3:18–19)

> For all have sinned, and come short of the glory of God. (Romans 3:23)

> For the wages of sin is death. (Romans 6:23)

The plain biblical fact of the matter is that humanity is guilty from birth. Romans 3:23 says that "all have sinned and fall short of the glory of God." *All* is an inclusive word. The deep and mysterious meaning of the Greek word *all* is *everyone*. Everyone— every person on the planet—is guilty from the beginning. Thus, in reality, if no one ever heard the gospel, and a person never had the chance to come to Christ, he is still condemned—already. He is guilty before God and deserving of hell, or eternal *death* (Romans 6:23), *from the start.*

This is not a matter of unfairness on God's part. God is holy, and humankind is sinful. God did not leave man; man left God. Not one of us *deserves* to come into His presence and live with Him in heaven—not one. If we never heard the gospel, we would be no worse off than we were from the beginning.

We are already sinners in the presence of a holy and righteous God, and we *deserve* hell. The secular worldview goes nuts over this assertion. Remember, secularists elevate humans to the highest order. We are the captains of our own destiny, they say. *We* are god. The secular worldview cannot abide the fact that man is *deserving* of hell.

THE GOOD NEWS

The good news is that the gospel *is* going out, and billions are coming up against it and having to make a decision about Jesus' claim upon their lives. A loving God is giving them a loving chance. In the grand scheme of things, God does not have to give *anyone* a chance. Nevertheless, He does, because He loves us and desires to redeem His creation. Those who respond to His offer of salvation, He receives.

Think of the love of God! He does not *have* to offer salvation to a single person. He did not *have* to send His Son. He did not have to bear the burden for our sin. He does not have to offer a way for fallen humanity to be redeemed, but He does.

The fact that He *would* offer salvation to one person out of seven billion would be a supreme act of love, mercy, and grace. However, in His infinite love and mercy, God offers His salvation to *whosoever will* (John 3:16). God is unbelievably gracious.

The proclaiming of the gospel to the world by the biblical church of Jesus is a monumental task and assignment—for which God will hold us accountable. This is why the book you are reading has been written, that you may be competently equipped to declare the gospel and the mysteries of life in an accurate, scientific, and contextual manner.

> Study to shew thyself approved unto God, a workman that needeth not to be ashamed, rightly dividing the word of truth. (2 Timothy 2:15)

Thus, as hard as this truth may be for a number of people to accept, it is an eternal and biblical truth. Humanity is guilty. Our sin nature condemns us from the beginning. Therefore, the people of God must have a heart and a passion for reaching the world for Jesus. The dread of it is that we are being held accountable when we have the opportunity to proclaim the truth of the gospel but do not.

THE THIRD FALSE ASSUMPTION: IT IS IMPOSSIBLE FOR EVERYONE TO KNOW THE TRUTH

The next false assumption involves the charge of *unfairness*, Those who subscribe to it think that God is unfair because not everyone will get to hear the gospel preached. In fact, they say, God Himself cannot reach *anyone* with His truth without the assistance of someone else. This is not the case. Of course, the biblically prescribed and preferred way for the world to be reached with the gospel of Jesus is for people to tell other people. We call this work the ministry of *evangelism*, outreach, or missions. This was Jesus' command to His disciples right before He ascended into Heaven.

> And Jesus came and spake unto them, saying, All power is given unto me in heaven and in earth. Go ye therefore, and teach all nations, baptizing them in the name of the Father,

and of the Son, and of the Holy Ghost: teaching them to observe all things whatsoever I have commanded you: and, lo, I am with you always, even unto the end of the world. Amen. (Matthew 28:18–20)

We have no doubt of this clear command. However, this is not intended to suggest that God is limited by man's disobedience. This is a command from the head of the Church—Jesus. His orders are that *we* are to take the gospel to the world. If we do not, we are forever held accountable.

Even so, let me assure you, God is *not* limited by our failure or disobedience. He will never wring his hands in anxiety saying, *"What shall I do? How will I save anyone? My people have not taken the message to the world."*

Do you remember Moses being reached by God? God appeared to Moses in a burning bush on the remote, uncharted backside of a desert. God did not need a missionary to reach Moses. He merely reached down and selected him. God delivered the message Himself. With what was Moses then charged? He was charged with taking God's message of *salvation* back to the children of Israel and to Pharaoh himself. God reached down to one man, and through that one man, He made available the salvation of millions down through the generations.

Do you remember the apostle Paul? Long before he was known as Paul, he was known as the Pharisee Saul. He hated the Christian sect that had emerged within the Jewish synagogue, and was determined to do God a favor and eliminate all of those Christian "heretics." God had other plans. Jesus did not wait for a particular man or missionary to reach out to Saul. In a blaze of glory, Jesus did it Himself (Acts 9). He then sent a man, named Ananias, to Saul to minister to his needs and to disciple him.

With what assignment was Paul charged? He was charged with taking the message of God's salvation to the world of the

Roman Empire. He did it with boldness and faith. God personally reached down to one man, and through that one man, He provided for the salvation of millions down through the ages. Does this sound familiar?

A myriad of parallel anecdotal scenarios exist coming out of modern mission work around the world. Missionaries consistently report supernatural tales told among remote people groups of how God Himself revealed His Word and truth to them.

Several tell of a "clear gospel message" that related to their tribe or community. I have no way of verifying these accounts, but the anecdotes do exist. However, I know the truth of God's Word. I know the Bible relates that, at times, God employed angels to declare His message to mortal men.

Understanding this particular truth, though, does not relieve the Christian church of taking the gospel to the world. That is our high calling. We are the Moses and Paul of our day. If you are a born-again believer, then *you* have been set apart to take the gospel to your world. The call to reach the world with the good news of salvation is the *mission* of the church.

But let us never think that God is somehow *unfair* because a missionary failed to go forth, a church failed to send, a Christian failed to witness, or an outreach ministry did not respond. God is not limited by our unwillingness, disobedience, or failure. God is not powerless, and He is not unjust.

At this point, we return to the question posed by our atheist friend: *What about the people who have never heard?*

This question is meant to cripple our gospel presentation and reduce the gospel delivery system to an unfair and incompetent proposition. It is intended to reduce God Himself to an unfair "Magic Man in the sky." However, nothing could be farther from the *true truth.*

As already demonstrated, God is capable of reaching whomever He chooses, whenever and wherever He chooses. Yes, our mission is to deliver the gospel, and we will answer for our success or failure to do so. However, if a person *never* hears the gospel *at all*—that eternal matter must be left to God. I am certain He knows how to straighten out the matter. His ability and fairness are not limited by anything that *we* do or choose not to do.

Therefore, the argument that the unbeliever makes in this regard goes down in flames. It is not legitimate; neither is it biblical.

The unbeliever may not care for these answers. He may balk at their profoundness. Nevertheless, answers *exist*, and now *you* understand them. Do not be afraid to respond with the truth, regardless of the unbeliever's vitriolic response, for the fact of the matter is that, in an unimaginable act of grace and fairness, God reaches out to *all* of us.

This now leads us to another matter of biblical truth that the unbelieving world often hates to hear us proclaim. Let us examine whether or not we are really living in the *end-times*.

· 20 ·

THE SKY IS FALLING!
THE SKY IS FALLING!

Christians seem to have this annoying little habit of talking incessantly about the end of time.
There shall come in the last days scoffers, . . . saying, Where is the promise of his coming?
—2 Peter 3:3–4

T he story is told of a traffic-laden highway through a short desert stretch in New Mexico where a peculiar little preacher named Nate Johnson walked every day, shouting and preaching to the many people who roared past in their cars. *"Repent, for the end of the world is near!"* was his unwavering outcry.

One night, as he walked, he came across an unusual object. Nate was certain that God Himself had placed this oddity in his path. Just off the edge of the road before him was a gigantic red lever. It was illuminated in the night by an eerie, heavenly glow. The lever had a large sign on a white background with enormous, red-letter print. The sign's message declared: PULL THIS LEVER TO END THE WORLD.

Nate saw this as the perfect spot for him to preach. He was overjoyed that the Lord provided him with such an attraction and such an obvious sign. Nate thought that God was smiling upon his work.

Soon, several automobiles were parked all around him. Eventually, they were parked up and down the road. As more time passed, people were walking over a mile behind the growing line of parked cars just to observe, photograph, and discuss the oddity of the preacher and the lever. Many were powerfully moved by the convincing presentation of his prophetic messages.

All seemed to proceed well until, after some time, so many people and so many cars accumulated that the road was nearly blocked.

Late one afternoon, a large semitruck came barreling down the highway. As the rig topped the hill and bore down on the crowded road overflowing with scattering people, the driver realized he could not stop in time. The driver had a horrendous decision to make: run over Nate or run over the ominous lever. Those were his only options. The driver pointed his 18-wheeler straight toward Preacher Nate.

As the big-rig driver explained to the highway patrol later, he felt he had no other option, given the gravity of his choices. Pointing to the smudge spot on the road that used to be Preacher Nate Johnson, the truck driver declared, *"I figured it was better Nate than Lever."*

This is amazingly similar to the frequent response of the secularist to one of the clear messages of the Word of God. That message is: *"A day of judgment is coming."*

The Bible has placed several *red levers* right in the middle of life's path. These red levers serve as warning signs that the Lord's wrath and judgment *are* coming upon the world.

Predictably, the secularist often attempts to merely run over the bearer of the message. He would rather do that than deal with the large red lever in the middle of his path and the possibility that the message may have veracity.

One of the objections of the unbelieving world to the overall Christian message is that Christians seem to have the annoying little habit of talking incessantly about the *end of time*. A number of them claim the end is imminent.

You might ask, what are the large red levers in the middle of the path? In reality, they are before our eyes every day. They are recorded in the Word of God through prophecies that are thousands of years old. Yet, many of the prophesied events have never occurred in the totality of the history of humanity—until *our* generation. Before I discuss these particular *levers*, let us first secure a solid biblical understanding of the contextual truth of the *last days*.

THE TIME OF THE END

The terms *last days, end of the age, last times, time of the end,* and *day of the Lord* are all biblical terms. These terms are not merely little catchphrases that sensational preachers have made up in order to scare people into heaven. They are declared in the Word of God as biblical truths, and their biblical uses are plentiful.

If these words and the ideas they convey are in the Bible—and they *are* there in copious amounts—then should not the contextual understanding and preaching of these truths be included in our message to the world? Of course they should. However, we must first understand the meanings of these words within their biblical context.

Let me begin by giving an example of each of these phrases from the Word of God so you may see that they are there, in the Word, in the context of which we speak.

Last Days

Knowing this first, that there shall come in the last days scoffers, walking after their own lusts, and saying, Where is the promise of his coming? for since the fathers fell asleep, all things continue as they were from the beginning of the creation. (2 Peter 3:3–4)

Time of the End

And he said, Go thy way, Daniel: for the words are closed up and sealed till the time of the end. (Daniel 12:9)

The Last Times

But, beloved, remember ye the words which were spoken before of the apostles of our Lord Jesus Christ; how that they told you there should be mockers in the last time, who should walk after their own ungodly lusts. These be they who separate themselves, sensual, having not the Spirit. (Jude 17–19)

The Day of the Lord

But of the times and the seasons, brethren, ye have no need that I write unto you. For yourselves know perfectly that the day of the Lord so cometh as a thief in the night. (1 Thessalonians 5:1–2)

The End of the Age (World)

And as he sat upon the mount of Olives, the disciples came unto him privately, saying, Tell us, when shall these things be? and what shall be the sign of thy coming, and of the end of the world? (Matthew 24:3)

The Truth of the Coming Judgment

For when they shall say, Peace and safety; then sudden destruction cometh upon them, as travail upon a woman with child; and they shall not escape. (1 Thessalonians 5:3)

What do these words mean? They speak of a time in the future of humankind when everything we now know will *end*. What does that mean? Is the sky *really* falling?

In reality, when understood in context, the message that *all things as we now know it will eventually end* is a message of comfort and encouragement to the Christian. The Word of God clearly states this truth. Further, we are encouraged to work and pray to *speed the coming* of the last days. Consider the following scriptural truths:

For the Lord himself shall descend from heaven with a shout, with the voice of the archangel, and with the trump of God: and the dead in Christ shall rise first: Then we which are alive and remain shall be caught up together with them in the clouds, to meet the Lord in the air: and so shall we ever be with the Lord. Wherefore comfort one another with these words. (1 Thessalonians 4:16–18)

Seeing then that all these things shall be dissolved, what manner of persons ought ye to be in all holy conversation and godliness, looking for and hasting unto the coming of the day of God, wherein the heavens being on fire shall be dissolved, and the elements shall melt with fervent heat? (2 Peter 3:11–12)

How can the *end of time* be a desired occurrence for the Christian? Are the last days something we should anxiously anticipate? Without a doubt, these words are ominous to the one who does not fully understand the truth of God's prophetic message. That is why we must hastily take the gospel to the ends of the earth. Time is growing shorter with each passing day. However, to the born-again Christian who is given glimpses of the glory that is to come, the promise of the end of time is a glorious thing.

Why is it so glorious? Because the *end of time* refers, very specifically, to the end of *man's* time—and to the beginning of *God's* time, or God's day. When humanity's corrupted, hateful, sin-filled, and godless historical reign on earth is over, Jesus' reign of peace, righteousness, and bliss will commence, and it will continue forever.

Consider this scenario for a moment: If you could snap your fingers right now and end all death, pain, suffering, crime, corruption, pollution, wars, murders, rapes, thieving, lying, destruction and terrorism—would you? Absolutely, you would. Who would not wish for such a world?

God's Word declares that this day *is* coming. If you belong to the Lord, why would you not want this day to come soon— even today?

The message of *the last days* is one of gloom and doom only for those who scoff. It only points to despair and disdain for those who are lost. It is foolishness for the fish in the pond to think no other reality of existence can be true because they cannot see it or imagine it.

Of course, the atheist, the evolutionist, and the secularist will laugh at our insistence that this *day of the Lord* is coming. They are swimming around in their fishpond, happy within their little world of reality and duly impressed with their self-proclaimed brilliance.

Nevertheless, no amount of denying will stop the plan and purpose of God. He will have a new creation. God will bring heaven and earth together under one head, Jesus Christ. His new world will be populated with those who have passed the test, graduated boot camp, believed, and trusted, because they chose to follow the way of Jesus. It *will* happen—count on it.

THE CERTAINTY OF THE MATTER

The certainty of the matter is sealed by the already-accomplished prophetic events of God's Word. Let me explain.

We have had the Word of God in our possession for thousands of years. We have had many opportunities to discern its accuracy and truthfulness. Other than the prophecies of the last days, or the *day of the Lord,* numerous other prophecies have been specifically fulfilled in ages past.

We have predictions of kings, kingdoms, nations, events, and coming disasters upon certain peoples. We have oracles about wars, uprisings, births, and deaths of particular individuals.

History bears out the veracity and the fulfillment of these foreshadowings in exacting detail. Likewise, we have dozens of prophecies about the *first coming* of the Christ. They specifically foretold of His place of birth, time of appearance, words of His ministry, miracles He would perform, His vicarious death, the brutal nature of His crucifixion, and even His resurrection and ascension. As noted in a previous chapter, all of these predictions were fulfilled to the letter in the person of Jesus Christ. In other words, we can trust His Word!

If we can trust His Word because of the testimony of truthfulness based on those prophecies that have already been fulfilled, then does it not make sense that we can trust His Word concerning the ones that are yet to be fulfilled?

Scores of prophecies exist, from Genesis to Revelation, about the *second coming* of Jesus, the rapture of the church, God's outpouring of His final wrath upon the world, and the coming of a new earth and a new heaven—a recreated paradise. No logical reason exists to assume that these prophecies will not also be precisely carried out. We can speak with assurance about the end of time (human rule) because the Word of God speaks incessantly, with confidence and clarity, about such things. We trust His Word. It is that simple.

HAS NOT *EVERY* GENERATION BELIEVED THAT IT WAS IN THE END TIMES?

Evidence suggests that almost every generation since the time of Jesus Christ has imagined itself to be the generation of the *end*. Forever, a preacher has been preaching some message to some group that the time is not only near, but the time is *now*!

Several detractors of the biblical message have attempted to prove that the New Testament documents cannot be the infallible Word of God because, undoubtedly, Peter, Paul, and John, seemed to think the end was coming in their lifetimes. Yet the end did not come. They were mistaken, the critics would say, and therefore, since the disciples were wrong, the Bible is wrong.

This can initially appear as a powerful argument. In reality, however, it is flawed, for not one of these biblical writers named a specific day or time when the end would come. When their actions are examined in proper context, they merely called their generation to readiness.

They did this because they did not know with any degree of certainty when the time of the end would come. The majority of the biblical signs we look for today, to discern the times in which we live in relation to the end, were given by the New Testament writers themselves. Evidently, if they knew the signs to look for, they were looking for them to happen in their lifetimes as well. Yet, none of those particular signs materialized within their lifetimes. They were looking for them, hoping for them, and making themselves ready for them. Therefore, so should we.

Before we move to the signs, or the *levers*, that have been fulfilled in our lifetime, thus giving us the ability to proclaim with confidence that the end of time is very near, let us deal with an oft-misunderstood passage of scripture. Cynics often use it to indicate that somehow even Jesus Himself was mistaken about the *end-of-time* prophecies:

> For the Son of man shall come in the glory of his Father with
> his angels; and then he shall reward every man according to
> his works. Verily I say unto you, There be some standing here,
> which shall not taste of death, till they see the Son of man
> coming in his kingdom. (Matthew 16:27–28)

At first reading, we may think Jesus was clearly in the wrong.
He thought those disciples who were standing with Him were
going to see Him return in His glory before they died. The Bible
critic would argue that since the disciples did not see this happen,
then Jesus was incorrect.

If Jesus was mistaken, then He cannot be the Son of God and
the Savior of the World. If this is true, they continue, then the
New Testament documents are false and present a false message.
This is a powerful argument; would you not agree?

Let not your heart be troubled though. The detractor's
interpretation of this passage is incorrect and out of context,
and it ignores the next verses. What else would you expect from
a person who sees life exclusively through a secular worldview?
So then, you might ask, what *is* the proper context and interpretation of this passage?

Jesus did not say one word here about the end of time or
the day of the Lord or the last days—not one word. What Jesus
did say was that some who were standing there would see Him
in His glory before they died. The following verses display only
one of three major fulfillments of this marvelous declaration.

> And after six days Jesus taketh Peter, James, and John his
> brother, and bringeth them up into an high mountain apart,
> and was transfigured before them: and his face did shine as the
> sun, and his raiment was white as the light. (Matthew 17:1–2)

Jesus kept His promise! Within six days of uttering those prophetic words, they were fulfilled. Three of his disciples saw Jesus in His Glory as He was transfigured right before their eyes. They received a glimpse of glory even before they tasted of death.

They would receive two more such glimpses, for a total of three. First, they would see His resurrected and glorified body three days after Jesus' crucifixion. They would also witness His glorified state as He rose into the clouds and back to the Father at His ascension. Therefore, when Jesus spoke these words from Matthew 16, He meant them. They were not a mistake; Jesus did not lie. The disciples had not tasted of death, yet they saw Jesus in His glory. Do not let an unbeliever take this stunning passage of scripture out of context and with it, attempt to sidetrack you.

THE LEVERS ON THE SIDE OF THE ROAD

The levers on the side of the road are numerous. They are those prophecies that speak in a very specific manner of the *time of the end*, using prophecies that have already been fulfilled or are in the obvious process of being fulfilled. What of the argument, however, that every generation has thought they were living in the last days?

While that may be true, several of the same prophecies for which the generations before us looked have been fulfilled in *our* lifetime, and *only* in our lifetime of history. Let us discuss a few of them.

At the outset, we have the fulfillment of the return of Israel as a nation, which we discussed in a previous chapter. This is a huge one. I am convinced that the countdown clock started with this event.

To review briefly, because of their sin, Israel was punished and scattered, dispersed among the nations for more than two thousand years. The scattering and eventual return of Israel were first predicted by Moses sometime before the children of Israel set foot on the Promised Land.

As one moves through the Old Testament pages (for example, through Ezekiel's "dry bones" narrative, quoted earlier), one finds this recurring theme: *Israel will return to the land as a geographical nation in the last days.* Hosea 3:4–5 foretells:

> For the children of Israel shall abide many days without a king, and without a prince, and without a sacrifice, and without an image, and without an ephod, and without teraphim: Afterward shall the children of Israel return, and seek the LORD their God, and David their king; and shall fear the LORD and his goodness in the latter days [the last days].

The truly incredible thing is that while God's people waited for Israel's return to the land, centuries passed, and it did not happen. Numerous biblical commentators and preachers of the Word surmised that this impossible prophetic event could only happen *after* the return of Jesus, when He would set up His literal rule on the earth. They deduced: *How will millions of Jews who have been scattered throughout the nations return to the land and re-create the glory of former Israel?* They declared it impossible. Thus, they waited.

Then it *did* happen. On May 14, 1948, Israel declared its independence. Millions upon millions of Jews from all over the world have streamed back to their homeland. They continue to return. They are now a major nation and a major superpower with which to be reckoned. They are the daily focus of geopolitical and world attention, as well as the central player in day-to-day Middle East affairs. Israel is back! In the last twenty-five hundred years of human history, we are the *only* generation to see this prophecy fulfilled. I believe Israel's return is a clear sign that we are now in the last days.

MORE LEVERS

Nevertheless, Israel is not the exclusive sign of the *end-times*. Other signs will appear, and still other levers are every bit as clear and just as certain. Consider this verse from Matthew 24, when, in response to His disciples' question about the end of times, Jesus listed the certain signs of the last days:

> And this gospel of the kingdom will be preached in the whole world as a testimony to all nations, and then the end will come. (v. 14)

This is a clear declaration; do you agree? Consider the fact that when Jesus spoke these words, the gospel was not complete. Jesus had not gone to the cross; He had not risen from the grave or ascended into heaven. The Great Commission of reaching the world with the gospel had not been given.

Consider the fact that man had not discovered the *whole world*. The technology to take the gospel to the whole world was not available. Yet, Jesus claimed that when you see the completed gospel going forth via massive communication technologies to the whole (once it was discovered) world, then you will know the end is upon you.

We are the *only* generation in the last two millennia to see this occur. In fact, we only possessed *world-reaching* global communications technologies within the last several decades.

Today, the gospel *is* going to the entire world. The book you are reading is a small part of the fulfillment of that prophecy. The clock continues to tick.

Along these same lines, the Bible speaks of astounding technologies that could not have been imagined when it was written, including one that would enable the *whole world* to observe things together—and even to hear the gospel—at once. A different hi-tech miracle has enabled the scattered Jews from all over the world to return, *en masse,* to Israel. These biblical prophecies also take into account a worldwide marking system that the antichrist will use in the last days to determine who can buy, sell, and work. All of these inventions were nonexistent when the Bible first spoke of them. They must have seemed to be impossibilities.

Today we routinely use televisions, radios, the Internet, and satellite TV. Credit cards, computer chips, GPS, and cell phones are part of our everyday life. Watching news events unfold live and in real time on an hour-by-hour basis is mundane to us. Jet airplane and high-speed interstate travel are routine. We do not give them a second thought, because we live in a world where all of these technologies are being used to one extent or another. We are the *only* generation in human history to see these things happen. Yet they were foreshadowed in the Bible thousands of years in advance. The clock continues to tick.

I must not leave out the astonishing prophecies of Ezekiel 38 and 39. These prophecies, written more than twenty-five hundred years ago, speak of astonishing and never-before-seen alignments of Russia, Iran, Turkey, and Libya, along with certain other Middle Eastern and African nations that will join together and attack Israel in the last days.

The prophecy declared that Israel would be strong and back in the land when this attack happens. We have experienced a returned and strong Israel. Even now, the predicted enemy nations are beginning to form their alliances, and they are breathing out their threats and amassing nuclear weapons for the stated purpose of attacking Israel.

And again, we are the first and only generation to see it. *Ticktock, ticktock, ticktock* . . . I think you understand the point.

THE CONCLUSION OF THE MATTER

When Christians speak of the end of time or the last days, we do so because the Bible does and because we are commanded by the Word of God to do so. Prophecy is a large part of the biblical message. I understand the unbelieving world hates the message, but that does not make it less true. Before 1948, much of the Christian world could not fathom how Israel could return to their land, but they did. God's Word is always true.

When we speak to the unbelieving world of the soon-approaching judgment of God, we do not do so with glee, but with broken hearts and a sense of urgency. We understand that a number of fish in the pond will not believe or receive our message. We will proclaim it anyway. Some will believe; some will be saved. That is all we can do. God will do the rest.

Let us, as believers, take comfort in and be encouraged by the fact that the Lord will soon return. When He does, the end of wicked human rule will be upon us, and the beginning of Jesus' glorious reign of righteousness will commence. Let us encourage one another with these words.

Moreover, let us not forget this significant truth. Regardless of whether Jesus' return occurs in our lifetime or not, there will be an end to this worldly life sooner than we expect. We will all leave this world either in the rapture of the church or in the natural process of death. We will all appear before our Creator and give account of what we did with Jesus' claim upon our lives.

In the meantime, we watch. We must be ready. We must prepare for our future. On one hand, we must live our day-to-day lives as though Christ's return will not come for another thousand years. On the other hand, we must proclaim our faith and reach out to the world with zeal and passion as though Jesus could return at any moment. We are not allowed to set days or hours or to discern the exact date of His return, but we have been given distinct markers and signs. We *are* to discern the seasons. That day will not overtake His children like a thief in the night.

> [Jesus] . . . said unto them, When it is evening, ye say, it will be fair weather: for the sky is red. And in the morning, It will be foul weather to day: for the sky is red and lowering. O ye hypocrites, ye can discern the face of the sky; but can ye not discern the signs of the times? (Matthew 16:2–3)

> But ye, brethren, are not in darkness, that that day should overtake you as a thief. Ye are all the children of the light, and the children of the day: we are not of the night, nor of darkness. (1 Thessalonians 5:4–5)

Darkness is coming, and perhaps soon. Then again, we have the light. Do not let the Bible critic convince you to put it under a basket. Instead, together let us shine it into the coming darkness. It is our destiny.

· 21 ·

REQUIEM FOR A SAINT—
HOPE FOR A SINNER

W hen our journey began in chapter 1, we joined two college students on a resplendent fall day. They were on
campus, engaged in a philosophical and theological
discussion. The students, one an atheist and the other a Christian,
were debating the meaning and purpose of life.

You will remember that the Christian left the conversation
somewhat befuddled. Unfortunately, he did not garner much

help from either his pastor or his Sunday school teacher. The fictional pastor and Sunday School teacher and their insignificant advice were not meant as disparagements of pastors or teachers. Without doubt, numerous Bible teachers and ministers could have soundly answered the questions and the objections of the atheist's onslaught.

Others, however, could *not* have answered the questions with authority and contextual truth. A number of Christians are without this type of preparation. They have not equipped themselves to handle the Word of God for the world in which we now live. Christopher was not prepared. He had not read *this* book.

> Study to shew thyself approved unto God, a workman that needeth not to be ashamed, rightly dividing the word of truth. (2 Timothy 2:15)

> But sanctify the Lord God in your hearts: and be ready always to give an answer to every man that asketh you a reason of the hope that is in you with meekness and fear: having a good conscience; that, whereas they speak evil of you, as of evildoers, they may be ashamed that falsely accuse your good conversation in Christ. For it is better, if the will of God be so, that ye suffer for well doing, than for evil doing. (1 Peter 3:15–17)

Let us now consider that the Christian student, Christopher, had read this book and possessed a clear mental recall of its truths. Let us imagine that on that same gorgeous fall day, with its aureate beams of sunlight filling the campus commons, Christopher's defense of his faith went a bit differently this time.

Christopher said, "I would like to continue our conversation about the existence of God and His work of creation, if that is okay with you, Crowley."

"Look Christopher; here is the crux of the whole matter for me. I, for one, would rather believe in the observable, proven, and settled scientific evidence that abounds in our modern world, concerning the origins and obvious evolution of life, than to believe in some *magic man in the sky*, as you Christians do. I don't believe in God for the same reasons that I don't believe in the tooth fairy." Crowley tossed his head with finality.

"Hmm. It is interesting that you would immediately offer a straw man into our conversation," said Christopher, looking disappointed. "I have never claimed that God is magic, or a mere man, or that He lives in the sky. As a matter of fact, in all of our discussions, I have never come close to describing God in that manner. Clearly, nothing about my faith and position resembles a tooth fairy tale either. I feel you are being unfair by beginning the conversation this way. I have been told that when a 'straw man' is introduced into a debate, it is typically a certain sign that the one who introduces it knows his argument is weak and thus introduces a *substitute* argument. Would you care to rephrase your initial response?"

"But don't you *actually* say just such a thing?" Crowley said, wide-eyed. "Isn't that what you believe? Consider this: you always speak of the unseen and unobservable things that your God has done and continues to do. You talk about Him merely *speaking* things into existence. You talk about the mystical power of prayer and the magical, mystical *Holy Spirit* within you. You talk about Him living *up there*—wouldn't that mean the sky?—and you talk as if He were merely a bigger and more powerful version of humanity itself. In fact, Christopher, you are so vain as to refer to the human race as the *crowning glory* of His creation as if humanity itself were the be-all and end-all of everything that exists in the universe. Millions of species of life exist, yet you are so arrogant as to proclaim that humans are at the apex of the evolutionary chain? Isn't that true?"

"Yes, well, those are *your* characterizations of my faith," Christopher responded. "The contextual way I speak of those matters doesn't even resemble the way you have just stated it. But to be fair, let me address several of your deepest concerns here. As for the seen realities of life and the unseen presence of God and His power, the Bible speaks of these things, so do I. Are you suggesting that merely because we can't see or understand something, this *something* doesn't or can't exist? Surely you are not suggesting that an unseen reality or unseen force or power is mere *magic*. Consider the scientifically verified facts of quantum mechanics. We have unseen and unknown laws and functions that work at the quantum level every day. These forces and powers ensure our very existence, and they formulate the reality of the physical world in which we live. These same quantum laws also verify the incredibly real possibility of the existence of multiple dimensions of reality. Each dimension carries with it a reality that shapes and affects the other dimension. Some of this we already understand as factual. Undoubtedly, you are aware of these scientific truths. Hopefully, you don't refer to quantum mechanics as *magic*.

"I am not suggesting," Christopher went on, "that quantum mechanics is how God works or exists. I am only demonstrating the absurdity of suggesting that merely because we can't see something or don't understand something, somehow this proves it doesn't exist. On top of this, we have numerous examples from our own world of two realities existing side by side, yet one reality is not aware of the other. But, both *do* exist. Certainly, you don't suggest that the concepts of prayer, God, and unexplainable events we call miracles have absolutely *no possibility* of existence. If you *do* make this assertion, then you deny the truth of real science and real life as we know it. Why, my friend . . . that would be *foolish*. I believe you are much more intelligent than that. Let me share several illustrations that may help you. May I?"

Christopher continued the discourse by giving a detailed

accounting of the fishpond analogy, the anthill analogy, and the microbial-world analogy, explaining to his atheist friend that just as a student *looks down* through his microscope, God is *looking down* upon us, and at the same time, He exists all around us. All the myths of a *magic man in the sky* were being systematically dispelled by Christopher's treatise.

Crowley's mouth was hanging wide open as he listened to his surprisingly enlightened Christian friend. Suddenly, he was taking into account possibilities that he had never before considered. He began to internally question the dogma he had held for such a long time. He determined that he would speak to his atheist mentors about the perplexing discoveries he was making today.

As the two students rose from the bench and trekked to their next classes, the discussion continued. Crowley had grown a bit unnerved by the direction of the conversation. His head was swimming. What should he say next? He decided to take another stab at poking a hole in Christopher's Intelligent Design theory.

"Those are attention-grabbing illustrations," he said, "but you need to recognize that science deals only with the evidence before it. Scientific evidence has passed peer review and many years of excruciating scrutiny. When a mistake is made, it is corrected. When new evidence is discovered, it is examined and tested, then published for all to reexamine. This is the true scientific process. Again, this makes much more rational and reasonable sense than your proclamations of *faith* in something you can't even see."

"Ah, my friend," said Christopher, shaking his head, "I am afraid you haven't heard what I am saying. Again, you wouldn't suggest that quantum mechanics is not science, would you? We have mounds of theories arising out of our understanding of this science alone that deal with unseen things and forces. Yet, we say we are certain they are there because we see their influences. The same rationale holds true for the theory of gravity—and for the workings of God. But, let me also address another fallacy in your argument.

"You speak of science as if it has been settled in your atheistic favor, as if the whole process has now been perfected. Let me remind you that science has made several incredibly embarrassing declarations of so-called *truth*. And it claimed these 'truths' as *fact* for thousands of years before they were discovered as untrue and superstitious myths. Spontaneous generation is a superb example. I must admit that the vast majority of modern scientists still hold to some type of evolutionary philosophy. But a large number of highly degreed, published, and respected scientists, several of whom are academic and scientific prizewinners, dismiss much of evolution as faulty science. Many of these creation scientists hold numerous scientific patents and are leaders in their fields of research. They are credible and respected scientists. Therefore, the issue is far from settled in the *totality* of the scientific world.

"Furthermore," Christopher continued, "how do we factor in the number of scientists who *say* they follow the evolutionary model solely out of fear of losing face among their secular peers or losing their opportunities to publish their works or losing opportunities to secure federal grants to further their studies? If we were able to factor in these elements of the equation, I would imagine the number of so-called evolution scientists might be reduced by a significant number. We may never know this for certain, but this appears to be a reasonable assumption considering the overall selfishness of man and the harsh realities of life, government, publishing firms, and financial grants. If a specific trend, such as *intelligent design*, is not *politically correct,* powerful forces will work against that trend at all times to ensure it does not acquire a fair hearing. Such has been the case for various avenues of science throughout the ages. No, to categorically state that modern science has been thoroughly and fairly peer reviewed, scrutinized, vetted, and corrected when necessary, I am afraid, is not a fair or accurate statement. It just is not factual. Much has been written and catalogued to verify my assertion."

"Well, yes . . . of course," Crowley stammered. "I suppose . . . when you put it like that . . . but—"

"How else could I put it?" Christopher challenged. "Can't you admit science has proven that unseen realities and forces do exist? Hasn't science proven that multiple dimensions of reality, each affecting the other, do exist? Hasn't science proven that nothing living has ever been observed to arise from something that is nonliving? Isn't it a fact that real science is seldom settled but is continually in a state of discovery and refinement? Isn't it a demonstrated fact, as I have shown with the fishpond illustration, that two realities of flesh and blood can exist in the same world of reality, yet one is unaware of the other? The answer to all of my questions is yes. So again I ask, *how else could I put it?*"

"But, can you *prove* the existence of God?" Crowley asked. "No, you can't. Can you *verify* that He created anything? No—"

"Oh *yes*, my friend," Christopher interrupted. "I *can* prove both of these things. But you must be forewarned. The proof is irrefutable. Once you have been confronted with the truth, you will be unable to deny it, and you will be forever accountable before God with how you handle the truth. Are you willing to let me answer those two questions?"

"Well . . ." Crowley responded, with obvious trepidation, "yes. I am willing. I still don't believe that you can prove the existence of God, nor do I believe that you can prove He created anything. But I am willing to hear your proof. If you can prove these things, you will be the first to do so."

Christopher began to explain the proof of God through the nation of Israel. "Not only is this proof irrefutable," he concluded his report, "but it is also proof that God *created* something. He created one nation out of another, and He told the world that He would do it long before He actually did it. On top of that, He told the world the entire *future* of that nation, including its dispersion and ultimate return to the land in the last days."

"But, how do you *know* that your Bible and your religious beliefs are true?" Crowley insisted. "The only reason you believe it is that you were *raised* that way! What if you were raised in a remote place of the world? What if you had been raised to believe in some other religious system? I suppose you would be just as passionate about those beliefs as well. How can you say that *your* religion is the only correct one? The world has hundreds of religions. Aren't you being a bit arrogant to proclaim that yours is the *only* one that is correct? If you would stop and listen to yourself every now and then, you would be surprised at how silly all that Christian-ese sounds. It *is* unbelievable!"

"Again," Christopher countered, "the proof of God that I just presented to you is irrefutable and is enough in and of itself. God declared before He did *anything* with Israel that when He brought it all to pass, *this* would be His *proof* that our belief in Him was enough. However, on top of all that, there still exists the uniqueness of the biblical message and the Christian faith. Christianity stands alone and apart from all the other faith statements of the world. It is the only one with a unique relationship brought from God to man, and not from man to God." Christopher then expounded the differences in the Christian faith and the manufactured religious systems of the world. By the time he had finished, Crowley had hung his head.

"Look, my friend," Crowley said with a sigh, "in the past, I could not see what you see. But I will admit, I am beginning to see your point more clearly now. I have to say, that does make more sense to me, now more than ever . . . Can we continue this discussion tomorrow?"

"Of course," Christopher replied, smiling. "I would be honored. I will pray for you and for our discussion. I'll see you tomorrow."

Overwhelmed, Crowley shrugged his shoulders, turned, and walked away, thankful that his next classroom appeared before him just in time. He made his escape through the open doors, but as he took his seat, his thoughts spiraled.

Meanwhile, Christopher felt a deep and abiding contentment in his heart. The Holy Spirit of God testified to his soul that his work had been good today. He had fought a good fight.

DESPERATELY SEEKING ANSWERS . . . AGAIN

Having left his verbal exchange with Christopher and pondering matters he had not previously contemplated, Crowley vowed to present these same challenging questions to trusted mentors of his secular persuasion.

"I *told* you they were ignorant!" spat Richard, one of Crowley's more academic mentors. "They do not understand that the preponderance of scientific evidence supports our position. I *told* you not to bother talking to Christopher. Clearly, he is just brainwashed. Poor guy. He actually believes all that garbage. But don't you worry—the atheist is right; the Christian is wrong. Science supports us."

Hmm . . . thought Crowley to himself, as Richard blathered on. *I wonder . . . Am I so close-minded that I would believe there is no room for God in the entirety of all that is possible? How could I have been so closed to searching for real and total truth and at the same time consider myself so enlightened? Am I merely one of the unseeing fish in the pond? If so, I could be . . . so wrong.*

I can't wait until tomorrow.

***

Like Christopher, we must be able to present the truth with facts, understanding, and insight. We must be knowledgeable of the Word of God and its contextual truths. We must also immerse ourselves in competent understanding of the sciences and the world around us. This is a lifetime journey, but we must be faithful, and we must be willing to start *now*. This is the best the Christian can do.

When one becomes a Christian, we do not set our brains upon a shelf somewhere and memorize a handful of trite answers to the world's deep questions. When we have declared the gospel of Jesus with accuracy and defended our faith with competence, using reasonable illustrations along with the most accurate and updated scientific knowledge, then we have done our part as witnesses. We cover our conversations in prayer. We trust in the guidance of the Holy Spirit, speaking the truth of God's Word in a clear and plain fashion, in context and with accuracy, and the *Lord* does the rest. The process is that simple.

Our battle is not against flesh and blood. Rather, it is against unseen powers of wickedness and forces of evil, even in the heavenly (unseen) realms (dimensions). We are warriors in an oft-unseen battle.

But we are also the *seeing* fish in a pond full of *unseeing* fish, and we must warn them that a world of unseen but exceedingly real powers exists just beyond the surface and all around them. We do so because we have knowledge of a coming drought. The pond will soon be dried-up and dead, and all that we now understand as real will be made new.

When we speak of these things, we are often thought to be crazy, because many of the other fish cannot see these things. However, the other fish are wrong. We are right. Another world of reality exists just outside our pond. Thus, we tell them what we understand. What they do with it is now up to them.

We are certain of the reality of the coming judgment. We are certain of the salvation offered in Jesus Christ. With these truths in mind, we must bring light to a dark world. We must bring truth. We must bring the *good news*—the gospel of Jesus Christ. May many receive Him while there is still time.

> But if our gospel be hid, it is hid to them that are lost: in whom the god of this world hath blinded the minds of them which believe not, lest the light of the glorious gospel of Christ, who is the image of God, should shine unto them. For we preach not ourselves, but Christ Jesus the Lord; and ourselves your servants for Jesus' sake. For God, who commanded the light to shine out of darkness, hath shined in our hearts, to give the light of the knowledge of the glory of God in the face of Jesus Christ. (2 Corinthians 4:3–6)

> For I am not ashamed of the gospel of Christ: for it is the power of God unto salvation to every one that believeth. (Romans 1:16)

> Yet if any man suffer as a Christian, let him not be ashamed; but let him glorify God on this behalf. (1 Peter 4:16)

Thus, our journey has come full circle. God's light of truth now shines in our hearts. We now have the light of the knowledge of the glory of God. I urge you to take the light you have been given and go forth into the world of darkness. With this light, exalt the glory of God and lift high the gospel of Jesus Christ with boldness, without shame or hesitation.

Now we come to the ultimate question. This question eclipses all other questions a human being could ask. The answer to this monumental question has nothing less than eternal consequences.

· 22 ·

THE ULTIMATE QUESTION

More than likely, the majority of the readers of this book are born-again Christians who desire to add further knowledge to their arsenal of information in order to more effectively defend their faith. I pray this book has served you well in accomplishing that purpose.

In case you are *not* a born-again believer in Jesus Christ, perhaps this book has brought you to the understanding of your need for salvation. At this point, you may desire to know how to make certain you are saved. I have good news for you: the ability to *be certain* you are saved is a biblical promise:

> These things have I written unto you that believe on the name of the Son of God; that ye may know that ye have eternal life, and that ye may believe on the name of the Son of God. (1 John 5:13)

The ultimate question of life is: *Where will you spend eternity?* If the Bible is the Word of God, and if the God of the Bible truly *does* exist, then He has several significant and eternal things to say regarding this question. I believe the book you are reading has sufficiently proven the truthfulness of the existence of God, His uniqueness, and the veracity of the Bible as God's only true Word.

The message of God's love for you and His plan for your life are rather simple. God first wants you to understand that you *do* have a purpose in life. You are not merely the accidental, evolutionary descendant of a mysterious "common ancestor" and, thus, related to a chimpanzee. In reality, you represent the crowning glory of all that God has ever created. You were made to be unique—in the image of God Himself.

God desires your life to be lived here and now—full of meaning, purpose, value, and dignity. He wants to walk with you in a personal way through His Holy Spirit so that your life will be used to bring glory to Him and to reach others for His kingdom.

The Bible is clear that you cannot accomplish God's ultimate purpose for your life apart from His hand of grace. The reason you cannot accomplish this on your own is that you possess a sin nature. All of humanity is in this predicament of original sin. We are hopeless and lost; we are sinful beings. Within our core nature we have the tendency to reject the Word, the way, and the will of God as He has revealed it to us. And worse, the Bible declares that our unredeemed sin nature will keep us forever separated from the presence, love, and eternal home of God: "For all have sinned, and . . . the wages of sin is [eternal] death." (Romans 3:23; 6:23)

The message of hope, the *gospel* (or, the good news) is this: God has provided for your salvation. He has taken this great and astonishing, merciful, and gracious feat upon Himself, providing a way for you to be restored to Him in order that your purpose in life and eternity may be accomplished. Your sin nature has been atoned. It has been covered. It has been forgiven. This was done through the perfect sacrifice of Jesus Christ, the Son of God, God's exclusive plan of salvation for humanity.

> The gift of God is eternal life through Jesus Christ our Lord. (Romans 6:23)

> Neither is there salvation in any other: for there is none other name under heaven given among men, whereby we must be saved. (Acts 4:12)

> Jesus saith unto him, I am the way, the truth, and the life: no man cometh unto the Father, but by me. (John 14:6)

You must respond to God's offer of salvation in a personal manner. It cannot be *conferred* upon you. Salvation cannot happen to you only because you *believe* in God. You must personally call upon the name of Jesus to be saved, admitting that you are a sinner and in need of salvation. You must then proclaim that Jesus Christ died for your sins and believe that He rose from the grave in order to prove He is the Lord of life and the exclusive way of salvation.

That if thou shalt confess with thy mouth the Lord Jesus, and shalt believe in thine heart that God hath raised him from the dead, thou shalt be saved. For with the heart man believeth unto righteousness; and with the mouth confession is made unto salvation. (Romans 10:9–10)

Once you have settled this matter with God and have called upon the name of the Lord Jesus for your salvation, you can be assured of your inheritance in His kingdom, both in this world and in the world to come.

If you have not already done so, why not take this moment and pray to God for your salvation—right now? Why not call upon the name of the Lord Jesus Christ? You can settle this eternal matter now. The question of your salvation is the *ultimate* question of life.

For whosoever shall call upon the name of the Lord shall be saved. (Romans 10:13)

After you have asked Jesus for His free and gracious gift of salvation, confess Him before the world.

Whosoever therefore shall confess me before men, him will I confess also before my Father which is in heaven. But whosoever shall deny me before men, him will I also deny before my Father which is in heaven. (Matthew 10:32–33)

Seek out a Bible-believing and Jesus-honoring church family. Then arrange to publicly declare, through believer's baptism, that you now belong to the Lord.

And now why tarriest thou? arise, and be baptized, and wash away thy sins, calling on the name of the Lord. (Acts 22:16)

These are biblical mandates, and they are the first mile markers along your new journey and your redeemed life with your Creator. There is no greater joy, no grander purpose in life, than to be certain you are right with the God who created you, through a born-again relationship with Jesus Christ.

Welcome to God's eternal family!

NOTES

CHAPTER 5

1. Aristotle (ca. 343 BCE), *Book 5: The History of Animals*, transl., D'Arcy Wentworth Thompson (Oxford: Clarendon Press, 1910).
2. Aristotle [ca. 350 BCE], *Book 3: On the Generation of Animals*, transl., Arthur Platt (Oxford: Clarendon, 1912).
3. Clint Witchalls, "Biology Nobelist: Natural Selection Will Destroy Us," *New Scientist* magazine 28, no. 2801 (February 2011).

CHAPTER 7

1. "Definition of *abiogenesis*: a hypothetical organic phenomenon by which living organisms are created from nonliving matter," http://dictionary.kids.net.au/word/abiogenesis.
2. Billions of years ago, the planet Earth was a world destitute of living things. There was no flora, no fauna; the Earth was completely barren of life. Instead of having an atmosphere rich in nitrogen and oxygen, as it is today, the atmosphere on primitive Earth was composed primarily of methane, ammonia, hydrogen gas and water vapor. The lack of a protective ozone layer resulted in high exposure to UVB light and radiation. Earth was also extremely volcanically active in the past and was continuously out gassing chemicals into the atmosphere. Even the oceans of Earth were a primordial soup of chemicals such as ammonia, phosphate, nitrogen, and carbon. Generally, the world was not a hospitable place back then, at least not according to human standards.

   How did the Earth metamorphose from the lifeless planet described above to the world teeming with living organisms that we live on today? How could complex life have originated from non-living chemical elements? These are difficult questions to answer but scientists have developed a theory that describes how the very first microscopic life on primitive Earth could have evolved as a result of a series of chemical reactions. This theory is called chemosynthesis, and it describes the chemical evolution of cellular life. (Astrobiology: The Living Universe—Chemosynthetic Theory, "Chemosynthesis: A Theory for the Chemical Development of Life: Chemical Evolution through Chemosynthesis," http://library.thinkquest.org/C003763/index.php?page=origin04.)

3. James D. Mauseth, *Botany: An Introduction to Plant Biology*, 3rd ed. (n.p.: Jones and Bartlett Publishers, Inc., 2003), 517.

4. The Miller-Urey experiment simulated theoretical conditions which at the time were thought to be present on a prehistoric Earth. The prearranged conditions of the experiment tested for the possible occurrences of the chemical origins of life. Specifically, the experiment tested Alexander Oparin's and J. B. S. Haldane's hypothesis that conditions on the primitive Earth favored chemical reactions that synthesized organic, or living, compounds from inorganic, or nonliving, forerunners. The Miller-Urey experiment was considered the classic research on the origin of life. It was conducted in 1952 and published in 1953 by Stanley Miller and Harold Urey at the University of Chicago.

5. Charles McCombs, "Evolution Hopes You Don't Know Chemistry: The Problem with Chirality," http://www.icr.org/article/105/; available at http://www.icr.org/article/evolution-hopes-you-dont-know-chemistry-problem-wi/. Dr. Charles McCombs is a PhD-level organic chemist trained in the methods of scientific investigation and a research scientist who holds twenty chemical patents.

CHAPTER 9

1. Tim Folger, "If an Electron Can Be in Two Places at Once, Why Can't We?" *Discover* magazine, June 2005.

2. *Merriam-Webster Online*, s.v., "supernatural," http://www.merriam-webster.com/dictionary/supernatural.

CHAPTER 11

1. "Worldwide Adherents of All Religions by Six Continental Areas, Mid-1995" *Encyclopedia Britannica*, http://www.zpub.com/un/pope/relig.html.

2. Central Intelligence Agency, *CIA World Factbook*, https://www.cia.gov/library/publications/the-world-factbook/fields/2047.html.

3. "Part 8: Religion in American Life: The 2004 Political Landscape," Pew Research Center, http://people-press.org/reports/display.php3?PageID=757.

4. "AP/Ipsos Poll: Religious Fervor in U.S. Surpasses Faith in Many Other Highly Industrial Countries," 2005, http://www.ipsos-na.com/news/pressrelease.cfm?id=2694.

CHAPTER 17

1. The Pew Forum on Religion & Public Life, "Fighting over Darwin, State by State," February 4, 2009, http://pewforum.org/Science-and-Bioethics/Fighting-Over-Darwin-State-by-State.aspx.

CHAPTER 18

1. William J. Broad, "Maybe We Are Alone in the Universe, After All," *New York Times*, Science, February 8, 2000.
2. Peter D. Ward and Donald Brownlee, *Rare Earth: Why Complex Life Is Uncommon in the Universe*, 1ˢᵗ ed. (n.p.: Spring Publishers, 2000).
3. Broad, "Maybe We Are Alone in the Universe, After All."
4. Michael Denton, *Nature's Destiny: How the Laws of Biology Reveal Purpose in the Universe* (n.p.: Free Press, 1998).
5. Maya Pine, "The Genes We Share (A Report)," Howard Hughes Medical Institute, 2008, *A Robot That Tracks All the Genes in a Cell Reveals Key Patterns; Yeast Researchers Get a Head Start*, http://www.hhmi.org/genesweshare/a100.html.
6. Graham Bell, *The Masterpiece of Nature: The Evolution and Genetics of Sexuality* (Berkeley, CA: University of California—Berkeley, 1982), 19.
7. Julie Schecter, "How Did Sex Come About?" *Bioscience* 34 (December 1984): 680.
8. Bell, *The Masterpiece of Nature*, 54.
9. Mark Ridley, *The Cooperative Gene* (New York: The Free Press, 2001), 108, 111. Dr. Hugh Ross is one such scientist to calculate this probability.

ABOUT THE AUTHOR

Carl Gallups has been the senior pastor of Hickory Hammock Baptist Church since 1987. Since that time, he has preached to tens of thousands of people on three continents.

Carl has produced more than a dozen full-length documentary-style DVDs on various biblical subjects. Thousands of these DVDs have been distributed all over the world. Some of them have been translated into different languages.

He is a graduate of the Florida Police Academy, Florida State University (BS), and the New Orleans Baptist Theological Seminary (M. Div.) and served for many years as a member of the board of regents for the University of Mobile at Mobile, Alabama.

Before being called by God into full-time ministry, Carl had a ten-year career in Florida law enforcement. Since then, he has been the speaker in chapel services of the Southern Baptist Convention's Sunday School Board, New Orleans Baptist Theological Seminary, and the University of Mobile. He was also employed by the Southern Baptist Convention's Sunday School Board (currently LifeWay) for ten years as a youth evangelist. In this capacity, he was a regularly featured speaker for SBC-sponsored youth conferences conducted all over the United States and in western Canada. By special invitation, Carl was a featured speaker along with Dr. Josh McDowell at a "Right from Wrong" conference at the Ridgecrest Conference Center in Black Mountain, North Carolina.

For many years, Carl has written a weekly newspaper column, *Ask the Preacher*, for a northwest Florida newspaper, and he produces a weekly radio show by the same name, which is broadcast on a regional Gulf Coast radio station.

Carl has been a talk radio host since 2002. He currently hosts the highly popular *Freedom Friday with Carl Gallups Show* heard on 1330 WEBY AM out of Northwest Florida. The program broadcasts to four states along the Gulf Coast and has a large national audience by live stream on the Internet.

Carl is a popular guest commentator for radio interviews from coast to coast, and he consistently appears on hundreds of stations through syndicated program interviews. Carl has given several television interviews as well, including one for Canadian television.

In November 2011, Carl was a keynote speaker and conference leader at the Florida State Tea Party Convention and Republican Presidential Forum at the Daytona Beach Convention Center. Carl was the leadoff speaker for C. Edmund Wright, Kevin Johnson, and Pamela Geller.

Carl also produces contract videos and voice-over materials for several well-known online news sources. His voice, commentary, and opinions are known by millions around the world.

Carl has been married to his wife, Pam, since 1973. They have a son, daughter-in-law, and grandson: Brandon, Hannah, and Parker.